The Teacher's Guide to Changing Careers

Stories and step-by-step exercises to find the right role
and build a network to start a new life

by
Ashley Philipps

Copyright © 2024 by Ashley Philipps.

Layout & Cover Design: Mel Wise
Cover Photo/illustration: Mel Wise & Midjourney

Uploading or distributing photos, scans or any content from this book without prior permission is theft of the author's intellectual property. Please honor the author's work as you would your own. Thank you in advance for respecting our author's rights.

For permission requests, please contact the author at: ashley@teachingcareerchange.com

The Teacher's Guide to Changing Careers: Stories and Step-by-Step Exercises to Find the Right Role and Build a Network to Start a New Life

ISBN: (print) 78-1-940498-29-4, (ebook) 978-1-940498-38-6
BISAC category code SEL027000

Printed in the United States of America

Dedicated to any teacher that dreams of leaving the classroom.
I wrote this for you.
You are a talented professional, you can make a change.

Table of Contents

Get started however you like, but get started 1

Career Change Roadmap 3

THE JOURNEY OUT

Deciding To Leave Teaching (My Story) 7

You Are Unhappy, But You're Not Alone 17

My Journey Out and The Lessons I Want to Share with You 35

DISCOVERING YOUR FUTURE

Don't Say No (Setting Up Your Future for Success) 57

Develop a Growth Mindset and Find What Fits You 79

What's Possible? Discover Your Next Career 95

PUTTING YOUR PLAN TO ACTION

Building a Personal Brand and Telling a Story 119

LinkedIn, Resumes, Cover Letters, and References 139

Networking, Outreach, and Interviews 167

Success! Interviews and Advice From Teachers
Who Made a Career Change (And LOVE It) 191

LEARN THE LANGUAGE OF BUSINESS TO BUILD YOUR ACUMEN

Glossary 209

Acknowledgements 219

About the Font 221

Personal Statement (A Note on The Text) 223

Get started however you like, *but get started*

This isn't a traditional "business" book. It's not sterile and meant to look unopened after you've read it. It's not quite a self-help book. It's in between and it's meant for you to write in, write on, check off, highlight, underline, fold the pages, and circle back.

There are generous margins. Use them! Take notes, jot down ideas, mark info to look up or read again, and note questions you have.

This is your journey, and you are where you are. We can start there together.

If you've decided to leave teaching and you're all in, consider yourself tested out! Skip to Chapter Three. You'll still want to complete the exercise in Chapter Two. That's the foundation.

If you're not sure how you feel about teaching and need some time to reflect, start at Chapter One.

Maybe you want to leave but need some motivation. You want to hear about other people who made a successful classroom exit into a new career. Read Chapter 10 first.

Perhaps you want to answer the question, *if I'm not a teacher what else can I do?* Sneak peek Chapter Six. You won't be ready to complete the exercises as you'll need to read the previous chapters, but you'll love seeing how skilled and ready you are. There are so many options for you!

Chapters Four through Nine do build upon one another, but reading ahead is not a crime. Come on, you wish your students would read ahead! There is nothing wrong with gathering more information.

What does matter is that you invest in yourself, trust that you are a professional, and allow yourself the understanding that you do have the skills needed to thrive in a corporate role.

The exercises are guided, but you're not turning this in for credit. You're engaging with the content so you can change your life and not just get a new job, but build a career where you feel fulfilled, empowered, and able to support the life you want.

I wrote a Glossary of business terms. You'll find it in the back of the book. It is meant to help you understand what I'm writing about in Chapters Three through

Nine. Bookmark this Glossary and refer to it often. You'll also notice that there are blank entries at the end of the Glossary. Those are for you. Add the words you don't know, Google them, and fill in the definitions.

Business acumen is important and relatively easy to understand. Just like new material for students, giving it some time and looking at it often will make all the difference. It will be helpful to go back and reference previous chapters as you read.

Last note: I cannot say a career transition will be quick or easy. It is a process and an investment in yourself. It will take time, effort, and energy. You gave yourself four years plus studied for an exam to learn how to become a teacher. A career change will not be a slam dunk just because you want it and spend a few weeks engaging with this guidebook. You won't (hopefully!) have to invest four years into a career change, but to say it won't take months would be deceptive. Stick with it.

Enjoy the journey. You can do this.

Career Change Roadmap

You Are Here: CLASSROOM TEACHER

THE JOURNEY OUT

1. **Deciding to Make a Change**
   How I knew it was finally time for a change.

2. **You're Unhappy But You're Not Alone**
   Change is scary, but staying is scarier.

3. **Navigating an Exit From the Classroom**
   How I left the classroom and journeyed into the corporate world.

4. **Setting Your Future You Up for Success**
   Suggestions for what you can (and should) be doing to support a change while still teaching.

DISCOVERING YOUR FUTURE

5. **Develop Business Acumen and a Growth Mindset**
   Overcome your fears and research what Industries & Companies are out there.

6. **Your Next Career Path**
   Discover what career and jobs are right for you.

7. **Developing a Personal Brand to Market Yourself**
   Develop your personal brand and determine how you can share your story.

PUTTING YOUR PLAN TO ACTION

8. **Resumes, Cover Letters, and References**
   Resumes can be a beast, but with the right mindset a resume can be conquered.

9. **Networking, Outreach, and Interviews**
   Applying online is not working. That's because the secret is in networking.

10. **Success!**
    Hear from former teachers who have successfully left the classroom and built careers they love.

Where You'll Be: YOUR NEW CAREER!

Get Started

THE JOURNEY OUT

1

Deciding To Leave Teaching
(My Story)

Have you ever cried at work? Me too.

And I used to get stuck here. Focused on the wrong things and complaining about the situation ad nauseam. But for me? Venting feels SO GOOD, even if the feeling is fleeting. And the number of times I feel good after venting FAAARR outnumber the bad. That's enough data for me.

HOWEVER...venting has never solved *my problems.*

SO...do it, but then focus on making real changes.

We are going to take this chapter to commiserate. I'll tell you my experience. Some might say I'm bitter, a few will say iT wAsN't ThAT bAd, but most will get it.

Were there good times? Yeah. But obviously not enough to make me feel like staying was the right option.

I hope you can see yourself in this chapter: the frustrations, the emotions, the chaos, the challenges, the negativity coming at you even though you're trying your best.

This is me venting, then you venting, so that next we can get to work.

notes

I can't recall the exact moment I realized I wanted to leave teaching.

I've thought about it. I've reflected, thought back through all the disappointments, the lows, and even some of the highs. I thought after being out of teaching for 10 years it would come to me—wake me up at three a.m. like a detail I couldn't remember from the day before (e.g., *what was the name of my neighbor two houses up when I was in fourth grade???* Tara. Her name was Tara).

It did not happen like that.

What I did conclude through my reflection is that it was not one moment or one event. Looking back, for me, it happened gradually. It was compounded by many things. Some small, some large. But what became startling was the realization that it began during my very first year out of college.

Here are some of the stories that stick out.

Exhibit A

Teaching year number one. Me? Doe-eyed. Energized. Excited. Organized. A pleaser.

I genuinely cared about my job, my school, my students. My classroom decor was immaculate and decorated beautifully, very inviting. I was ready to make a difference!

And the year prior doesn't count because I was only a Study Hall Monitor and gave up one of my off periods to teach a class. Like a Super-Duper-Student-Teacher situation.

So naturally, I was assigned to a really tough group. Give the newbie teachers the headaches the veteran teachers don't want, right?

Literally and figuratively TOUGH. Gang members. Rough home lives. Time spent in juvenile detention centers. More than a third of my full student roster had an IEP or 504 or needed ESL services. Several students were taking the course a second time in an attempt to earn credit. My class sizes were larger than the classroom set of desks and textbooks.

One student in particular was constantly giving me a hard time. Looking back, of course he did. The deck was stacked against him. He certainly didn't see me as his ally. And he treated his other teachers the same, I wasn't special or unique to him. A parent conference about behavior and more consequences was inevitable, but I didn't want him to fail even if he seemingly didn't care.

notes

I called home. The conversation couldn't have gone worse.

Mom was tired of the calls; apparently, I had waited too long. You never want to be teacher call number four or five home the week mid-term grades are posted. Mom was unresponsive to a plan; she was at her limit before the first quarter was over. I emailed the assistant principal (AP) I reported to. Gave him the run down and finished with Mom's reaction. I asked what I should do.

By now I'm sure you're thinking the back half of this story is going to be about my next interaction with Mom. Wrong! I had no idea what was about to ensue.

Later that evening, it was well after 6 pm, I was still in my classroom working. Of course I was. I was a first-year teacher. I had nothing. No syllabi, no rubrics, no handouts…I was pages ahead of the students in the textbook, never mind an entire chapter.

I was grading papers and writing lesson plans since I didn't have any from previous school years. The AP popped his head into my room and (I'm not kidding) said, "you sound too white." Looking up from my desk, I just stared at him. I remember vividly being speechless, not knowing what to say. He took that as a cue to come into my classroom, sit down in a chair, and continue his "mentoring." He advised, "you need to change who you are when you make these calls." Again, I just stared at him. With no verbal response from me, he went on to say "Like me? If it's a white family, I introduce myself as Michael. If it's a black family, Mikey. If they are Hispanic, I say Miguel." Further explanation went something like this: be their race/ethnicity so they trust you, otherwise the parent/guardian won't listen. Once you are "one of them" you can say what you need to and get less resistance.

I felt sick to my stomach. I have always valued being my authentic self and I happen to be a straight, cis, white woman. I wanted those around me to have the same privilege I had to be themselves. I wanted that for my students. I could not imagine a world in which I was looking to educate and empower young people on who they wanted to be and what they wanted to do and not be my authentic self. The world can be a crappy place. I wanted students to know they had the power to change the world around them for good.

Yes, there is comfort in group think in some ways, but pretending to be another race or ethnicity to find common ground? That is a non-starter for me.

I remember somewhere in the conversation asking him, how do I change "Ashley" to not be white? And thinking to myself, why wouldn't I want to be myself? I know my inexperience meant I probably could have communicated better with Mom; I'm

notes

sure there are better suggestions I could have made. Used other wording. Asked if calling back at another time would have been better.

Honestly, I can't even tell you what happened next or how the next communication to Mom went. But not once have I concluded that the Michael/Mikey/Miguel approach was right for me.

And yes, I did change the AP's real name. I'm not here to dox anyone.

Exhibit B

Getting thrown under the bus? Painful. Freaking hurts.

I was in year three. Teaching the same subject for the third time. Planning was getting easier. Project-based learning was working for me. It was fun! I had a solid syllabus, rubrics, and detailed instructions. It was a whole thing, very planned out. Most of the students did a good job and I enjoyed watching them grow and learn. About 10% of the students excelled beyond what I could have imagined and blew me away—and I loved it. At times, I learned more from them than they did from me!

And then there was the roughly 15% that remained.

Twins that I had in separate class periods, same subject and project assignment, turned in the EXACT same project. I mean, they took twinning to the extreme. It gets better, though.

Not only were the projects a carbon copy of each other, it's 100% plagiarized. The mass majority of the content was from Wikipedia. And yes, it was the oH-sO-LaZy *direct cut-and-paste*. Different fonts, inconsistent text sizes, and my personal favorite, leaving in the hyperlinks.

Turns out, it wasn't even the students who did it. It was their father.

A total disaster TRIFECTA.

As you can imagine, the parent-teacher meeting we had to have was tense.

There is no greater unease than a **parent** caught cheating. A flustered parent ain't great, especially in front of the other parent who has to hear about all the drama and that their partner engaged in this behavior. Or hid it from them. Whatever. The point is, the marriage drama can suck all the air right out of the room.

The twins' counselor was there, as was their principal, so it wasn't just me. I felt okay going into the meeting. The situation sucked, but I hadn't cheated. And even

notes

though the meeting was going to be uncomfortable, to me this was an open-and-shut case. The district policy for plagiarism was a zero-tolerance policy and the students caught would earn no credit for the assignment. Done. Easy. Move on.

But according to the principal, the family's group cheating was somehow less of an egregious error in comparison to my syllabus quality, daily instruction, and expectations (you know, things like no plagiarism and following district policy).

The principal bent to the anger of the mother and the embarrassment of the father, and the situation went from bad to worse. He let those parents go off on me. Yelling, flustered, and mean.

Fun fact, there is an Education God because after a nice berating from two sneering parents empowered by a weak principal, the counselor stepped in, said that was enough, and told me I could leave the room.

I still think fondly of her and will forever be grateful for her relief and I hope that principal and those parents are exhausted from pounding sand all these years.

And the twins' punishment? I mean, come on. You know how this ends. They got three weeks to redo the entire project, could earn full credit minus a 10-point hit on the assignment (making an A still possible), and I had to find time to grade them. So much for academic rigor.

Exhibit C

Fast forward two years. I was a team leader in a large social studies department in a new district. Glad to have an unpaid lead promotion and on a new campus, but I was tired. I was burning out. It was probably showing but I didn't realize it.

I had very few peers who cared about teaching the way I did. Time and time again, so many teachers, who were really good people personally and I enjoyed talking with, refused to give attention and time to metrics that mattered. Would not take time to design and put effort into creating relevant assignments. Didn't baseline student ability level. Used outdated lesson plans. Denied technology.

I'll say this about my teaching style:

> I ❧ Refused ❧ To ❧ Assign ❧ A ❧ Daily ❧ Worksheet ❧ From ❧ 1982 ❧ And ❧ Call ❧ It ❧ Teaching

notes

Students at desks filling out antiquated, busy-work-worksheets grind my gears like no other. It is not teaching. It never has been. It never will be. It's lazy. My tolerance for it? Zip.

This district was VERY chaotic, misguided by poor district and campus leadership, and politically a mess. At the time I was so bent out of shape over it, so frustrated at the apathy of so many teachers. Looking back, had I stayed, I can't say I wouldn't have succumbed to the same "leave me alone, none of this is worth it" style.

The best part of this story, you're wondering?

I worked my ass off, they didn't, and they got paid more because they were employed longer. Hooray!

Exhibit D

I love football. I'm not picking on it. For real. I will never not root for my Mizzou Tigers in the fall.

But at *almost* Every. Single. School between August and November, I got this:

> Enter my classroom during my free period or 10 minutes after student dismissal for the day, The Football Coach.
>
> Handy that I would be in my room alone. Like, weird this would never happen in the staff room or in the hallway.
>
> The ask was always the same: change my gradebook so their STUDENT-athlete could take the field on Friday night.
>
> Why was this proposition given? Because:
>
> - "Football is all the STUDENT-athlete has" and
> - "Said STUDENT-athlete promises to start participating in class and turning in work" and
> - "STUDENT-athlete already has two Fs in other classes and mine would be the easiest to change."
>
> What went through my mind during these exchanges?
>
> - No, it's not. You're enabling bad behavior and are selfish.
> - Laughable.
> - Mrs. Math teacher and Mr. English teacher showed you the door too, huh?

notes

My favorite was the request from one coach that I simply change the grade Thursday to earn Friday eligibility, and then just change it back on Monday morning. Gee, Coach!! That is just a super idea!!

Ugh, no, thanks. I have standards.

Is That All?

No. There is WAAAAY more. These are a few more stories from my past and I'm sure you have experienced the same, similar, or dare I say, worse?

- One school had ONE student copy textbook for a class with 25+ students in it.
- One charter school had an owning company that saw a child's education as an opportunity for profit. More money was spent on a few months' rent from the city on a crumbling building to the charter company than I made for an entire year's work.
- A teacher down the hall from me witnessed out of her third story classroom window students (in their school uniforms) assault and rob a man on the street before school. The teacher reported it to the principal; the principal said she didn't want to be involved and did nothing. NOTHING.
- Students brought guns to campus. One child for DAYS hid in his backpack the gun his uncle used to rob a convenience store.
- I was underpaid and still had to use MY OWN MONEY to constantly buy kids school supplies and FOOD.
- I had a principal question why my grades weren't submitted online on time. I had to remind her for the 983,123,563,472th time that the IT department… wait for it…still had not set up an account for me.
- I taught on campuses where gang violence threats got to be so severe and common that at the end of the school year, they just cut the days short the last 6-8 weeks and bussed everyone home early.
- I was on a "hit list" of teachers to physically harm on the last day of school.
- I dealt with state DFS and how *slow* any action took, if any was taken at all. I watched kids who needed support the most just not get it or not get nearly enough.
- Kids dealt with adult issues: pregnancy and abortion, coming out as LGBTQ+, bullying, and the absolute mess that social media is creating on campuses.

Deciding to Leave Teaching

notes

- I witnessed the harmful effects of student drug use. It is an epidemic adults choose not to see.

- Once I had a male teacher, in front of my entire class, ask if I came home the night before from a date. When I asked the department head for help, he laughed at me. When I then went to the assistant principal to report it, I was asked to take it in jest and told the students probably didn't even understand. This was in front of 16-year-old boys. Trust me, they got what he was alluding to.

- There were many other instances of student cheating, parents cheating, and parents doing their child's assignments. And when everyone was caught? Parents were just plain nasty and took all their embarrassment and frustration out on me.

- One district docked pay two days because I took a sick day on a "Blackout Day" prior to a holiday. Apparently you were not supposed to get sick on that day in particular and not only did I not get paid on my sick day, I couldn't be paid on the holiday either.

In Summation

Teaching wore me down. It broke my spirit and stole my enthusiasm and my passion.

And it's worth making clear, it was never really the kids. For me, it was the adults, the pick-and-choose policies of what to follow and when, the lack of support, and the lack of control.

Now What?

Let's do a little bit of self-help, some come-down-from-teaching therapy. Get it all out now, because, like I wrote when we started this chapter, this is it. We move on and up from here.

Below, record your story. There is no wrong way to do this. Full sentences, lists, bullet points, fragments. Cover your frustrations, your emotions, the hard times, what stole your passion and enthusiasm. No turning this one in, teachers. It's for your eyes only.

MY STORY.

These are my experiences. This is why I need a change, what I don't want for my future. *And maybe a few things I'll miss.*

2

You Are Unhappy, But You're Not Alone

"Ugh. I hate sitting in PD. It's such a waste. No one is going to do this in their classroom."

"Why is she the one presenting? She doesn't even do it in her OWN classroom."

"I cannot believe they are doing that AGAIN this year."

"Did you hear they made her department chair? I cannot believe that!"

"He talks way too much about what to do. His students aren't even that successful."

"It didn't work last year but here we go again…"

"I'm so tired of dealing with new methodology. It's confusing. I want the old grade system back."

"Can they make us do that? I shouldn't have to stay late."

Sound familiar?

And it gets worse.

notes

My ears always perk up when I hear teachers griping. Perk up may be too positive. A better description may be more like a constant high-pitched ringing in the ears.

Don't judge me. *Have you ever heard a group of teachers talk about teaching?* 😳

Every conversation between teachers sounds more like a peer therapy session than a conversation. It is almost never positive. And they all talk over each other, trying to outdo each other as to who has it worse. It's the world's worst competition with only losers in the end. A race to the bottom.

And if you witness this fiasco? Look to see if there is a non-teacher. You'll know they are the non-teacher because they can't get a word in edgewise. They'll be the one with the glazed-over boredom or shocked look that says, "what in the world?"

Do these statements seem callous or cold? Maybe. The other view is, who likes to hear constant complaining? I don't think teachers who are in the trenches truly understand how much they complain and ONLY talk about teaching. I'm serious. When I was interviewing teachers in my network and I'd mentored for Chapter 10 (to share their success story), almost all said the same thing. They now realize how much they complained and obsessed over teaching. They tell similar stories to the ones below of teachers they still talk with. Their thoughts are the same: *get out! I wish you could see the other side.*

Here are ten standard and true examples of why I say with gusto:

> **EVERYONE IS UNHAPPY.**

When Teaching Ruins a Vacation

In St. Croix with my husband, on a Saturday late in the summer, we went on a lil' booze cruise to a National Park that had a beautiful white sand beach and incredible snorkeling.

Sitting across from us on the boat ride back were two women, both teachers. Although they were huddled together going off about the first week reporting back to school, I would learn later they were strangers and had also met on this excursion. I gathered reporting back would be two days later, on Monday. Their significant others sat on either side of them, not part of the conversation. One husband was at least listening, shaking his head and looking disgusted. The other was completely zoned out. As the boat docked, I couldn't help leaning over and interjecting.

notes

"Ladies," I said. "I was a teacher too. And it sucked. If you want a career that gives you flexibility and the ability to make actual money, please connect with me on LinkedIn. I'd love to help you."

They were aaallllll over my offer. Well, turns out, not all over the offer of help, but to vent to someone else. Talking over one another about their woes. How bad it was. Everything sucked. A whole mess of words. From both of them. At the same time.

Indifferent principals.

Long hours.

Crappy benefits.

Poor facilities and cuts to resources.

Additional late nights for PT conferences.

And COVID...learning Zoom, lack of student engagement, apathetic parents, no support...

I was overwhelmed in less than 90 seconds of them speaking at *me* but a teacher in this state loses their social radar. Remember Cady Heron in Mean Girls? The part where she couldn't stop the words from flowing out of her mouth, the "word vomit"? It becomes that—no stopping it. Neither would even take breath. It was problem after problem after pain after woe. I looked at the disengaged spouse. He said quietly, "I tell her all the time—leave [teaching]." He looked like the perfect mix of disgusted-angry-sad. He was tired of the griping. He wanted a happy partner. A satisfied and fulfilled partner. One who didn't complain daily when leaving for work and when she came home. I mean, good grief. **This was their last day of vacation and here she was spending their precious last hours in paradise complaining about something out of her control, days away. Yuck.**

And when these two women finally paused to take a breath and make the barrage of complaints a conversation, they asked me what it was that I did. They leaned in with interest.

And then the question I always get: *but how did you do that?* **How did I leave?**

You Are Unhappy, But You're Not Alone

notes

When You Vent to Complete Strangers

I was at a Friendsgiving in San Francisco.

I had been out of teaching for less than two school years and living in the Bay Area for the same amount of time. Ironically, I didn't know most people at this Friendsgiving event, but I knew a few and that was plenty of reason to go. While there I met a friend of a friend of a friend's girlfriend. I asked if she worked at the same tech company or went to the same university as most of the people there. It turned out she did not, but she was an elementary school teacher.

I responded that I used to be a teacher too. Her eyes got big. The question peppering began.

> **You were?!**
>
> **How long did you teach?**
>
> **What did you teach?**
>
> **Where did you teach?**

And then it began. More Cady Heron word vomit....

> **I hate it. Well, I mean, I love my kids but...** [*here is where I started to zone out*].

I'm sure she said nothing I hadn't heard before and I'm very sure it lacked importance, was uninteresting, and certainly not unique. I did feel really bad for her. I did, but I hadn't even spoken for more than five minutes. Did she even realize this? Did she know this was no longer a conversation?

...I watched some guys play darts...she was still complaining...

...I nibbled at my appetizers...she was still complaining...

...I nodded, not because I agreed but because I didn't want to appear rude...

...I thought, "Whoo, boy, I'm glad my internal dialogue is private because this convo is the worst right now..."

She was still complaining...but then stopped.

I started to come to and make eye contact.

> **"And I just don't know where to get a different job. How did you do it?"**

When Your Finances Are So Strapped Money Is A Cause Of Constant Anxiety

I'm chatting over G-Chat (this was in 2015, ok?) with a former colleague.

I'm in the first few weeks of my new job, new career path; he is still in teaching. In fact, this was his first year teaching. The year prior he was in a student teacher-like capacity. This meant the school expected the same student and grading load, but with lower pay. 😜

> "What do you make [salary] now? If you don't mind my asking…"

When You're So Overworked That Family Friends Seek Help

A text thread. Please don't judge him for being a Jayhawk fan. We all have a weakness.

> Hey Round of 32 Mizzou fan….
> would you have some time to speak with my very good friend's daughter - she's early/mid 30s, looking to get out of teaching for probably the same reason you did.
> #1 issue is $$ (she is working 2 jobs - teaching and bartending just to get by.
>
> She would like to get into sales or maybe even enablement. Fantastic teacher. Super hard worker, very smart. You are my go to!

>> Yes. You can send her my #
>>
>> She can text or call I'll set up time to chat.

> And although I was excited Kansas lost, you didn't help me out, because then I had to listen to James brag about how it was AR who beat them!

> Ha!! You can't win

You Are Unhappy, But You're Not Alone

notes

Two days later

> Hello Ashley. Just doing a quick survey on what you like best…The Bowl Eligible Jayhawk football team or the National Champion Basketball team?
>
> Were you ever able to connect with my friend's daughter?

> I met with her. She's great. Gave her homework and will meet with her again

> Thank you for meeting her. I've known her since she was 2. Her dad is my BFF and I'm trying to help her make the leap

> MIZ

When You're So Down Your Friends Seek Out Help For You

A common phone call (most don't have this vibe and energy though). Joie brings that. 😍

And I've kindly summarized it for ya.

Me: Hey, Joie!

Joie: Assshlleeyyyyyyy!! Hi!
It's been so long....

Me: WAY too long. What are you up to these days?

Joie: Celebrating my 3-year work anniversary!!!
How are you?
What are you up to?

Me: Just living the dream, obvi...
OMG! You live where????

The Teacher's Guide to Changing Careers

notes

Joie: You mean we are neighbors now????
            Let's get dinner ASAP!

We banter and catch up (all the good love and energy).

And then, the ask:

Joie: *I have a friend.*
            She's in education and wants more from life.
            Can I introduce her to you?

When You Completely Lose Your Social Radar

I'm in beautiful Springfield, Missouri.

I am with my cousin who might as well be my sister and we are celebrating her 40th birthday. At a local brewery with good drinks, games, and atmosphere. A fun night. A happy night. It's just her and me. It's great.

And then her Spidey Sense goes off, she turns to a table near us, and before I know it, I'm surrounded by four elementary school teachers from her campus. And guess what? All griping about teaching.

> Bad principals, suck-up teachers and principal's pets, lack of resources…
>
> More before- and after-school duties for no pay…
>
> Blah, blah, blah.
>
> Blah, blah, blah, blah, blah, blah.

UGH to it ALL.

I'm making eye contact, but I am not at all listening to what I've heard hundreds of times.

My inner dialogue starts to take over…

I wonder if singing "Tale as Old as Time" in my best Mrs. Potts' voice would get them to stop the madness and barrage of complaining.

I want the birthday celebration back. We were having fun and for more than 30 minutes now, I've had to hear gossip and frustration over people I will never know and situations out of everyone's control. Where in the world is their social radar? Why act like this at a

notes

brewery, on a Saturday night? Their husbands are all laughing and playing lawn darts or something. Good golly. Enjoy life. But they can't. That's the problem.

And then I hear them: the questions.

> "How did you leave teaching?"
>
> "How much money do you make doing that?"
>
> "You can work wherever you want? How?"

When You're Burnt Out And Exhausted

In my inbox.

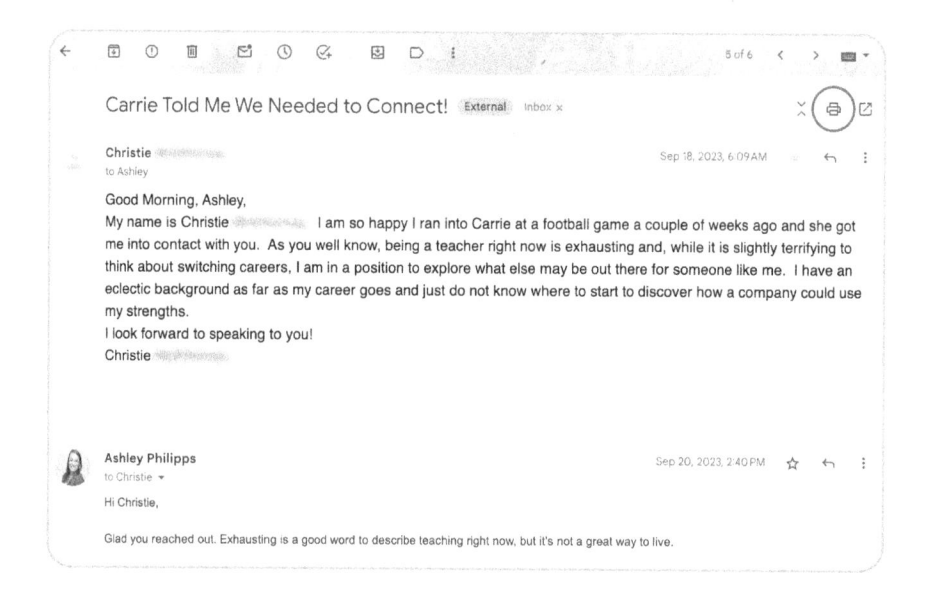

Carrie Told Me We Needed to Connect! External Inbox

Christie Sep 18, 2023, 6:09 AM
to Ashley

Good Morning, Ashley,
My name is Christie ▓▓▓▓▓. I am so happy I ran into Carrie at a football game a couple of weeks ago and she got me into contact with you. As you well know, being a teacher right now is exhausting and, while it is slightly terrifying to think about switching careers, I am in a position to explore what else may be out there for someone like me. I have an eclectic background as far as my career goes and just do not know where to start to discover how a company could use my strengths.
I look forward to speaking to you!
Christie ▓▓▓▓▓

Ashley Philipps Sep 20, 2023, 2:40 PM
to Christie

Hi Christie,
Glad you reached out. Exhausting is a good word to describe teaching right now, but it's not a great way to live.

When You Complain Enough Your Family Asks For Help On Your Behalf

A former coworker while I'm in job number two since teaching:

> Whuuuuuttt! You used to be a teacher!? My sister is a teacher and she HAAATESSSSSSS it. You gotta talk to her.
>
> Can you help her?

When You Can't Participate In Normal Life Due To The Schedule

I was in a Zoom meeting with a candidate for hire.

The role she is seeking is a Business Development Representative (BDR). It's a sales position, usually where folks start. And it can be a very lucrative one, especially at the right company selling the right solution at the right time in the market.

She had spent her hard-earned money on a self-paced training program for this EXACT role.

Nothing about that actually matters. Here is what does:

I rescheduled the interview more than twice due to interruptions during her planning period at school (Try getting a hiring manager that wasn't a teacher to be sympathetic and will deal with that. You won't.).

She was exhausted and looked it. I could see it in her eyes, even via a computer screen.

The deep, deep exhaustion.

She teared up talking about debt, bills, and lack of growth in teaching.

This job would change her life, what this salary would do for her and her two young children.

She couldn't risk leaving in the middle of the school year as her campus and district was so toxic she was fearful of repercussions, some real, some imagined.

She wanted out so badly but simply wouldn't leave her contract early. And so the job came and went.

It left me sad for days on end.

notes

When You Know You Want A Change But Not Sure What Direction To Take

LinkedIn Messenger. I get notes like these All. The. Time.

> • 8:34 PM
>
> Hey Ashley, hope you're doing well! I'm writing because I wanted to ask you for a favor. My friend is interested in making a change from teaching and I remembered you used to be a teacher as well and then moved over to sales enablement. I think this could be a good opportunity for her as well. She's worked in other fields before becoming a teacher and now would like to get back into the corporate world. Would you be willing to have a quick informational interview with her? She's actually not on LinkedIn yet but wondering if you wouldn't mind me making an email introduction? Please let me know. Thanks so much!

The question "how did I get out?" and *the ask* to support another's career transition is part of every conversation I have now when it relates to the teaching profession.

Even when speaking with co-workers in passing conversation, at an event, at a conference. If I mention I was a teacher, the response is almost always the same. Surprise, then a shared story of a person they know who is currently unhappy in the classroom and feels stuck, and then wonderment of how I got out.

When I connect with the teacher at the end of the ask, almost all will talk about lack of funding, school facilities falling apart, safety issues, communities that lack basic resources and are seemingly stuck in survival mode, favoritism among the staff, discipline issues, virtual madness, attendance issues, lack of professional benefits, pressure to do more with so much less, and insultingly low pay.

And I can relate.

Teaching is a thankless job. And yes, I'm encouraging you to leave. Some people, you know, *those teachers*, will get all pious on you. They'll be loud about how iT iSN't AbOuT tHe MoNeY or paid time off or work-life balance but are the same folks grumbling about low pay and the pain of sub plans and grading papers at

10:30 PM on a Wednesday night. They'll tout "summer break" as a premier benefit and say you are educating the future.

Ignore 'em.

Knowledge that you are helping "the future" won't pay your bills, let you live without roommates, go on vacations, or go out to dinner and drinks when you want.

It sure as Hades won't help you retire early. Or even retire without getting a part-time job. Or keeping that bartender job at 47 when you'd rather be home with family or out with friends.

And that career change comes with a new sense of pride. Fulfillment. Paid time off without a mountain of prep work. Flexibility. A living wage. Bonuses for effort. And if you pick the right career, it comes with perks like working remotely, paid maternity/paternity leave, technology that is not 20 years outdated, and opportunity to grow and advance your career.

Still not convinced?

Let me ask you this. Where else in your life do you make that many crappy excuses to continue to be miserable? My guess is not many. And if so, let's get you a different self-help book!!

> Are teachers important? Yes.
>
> Is the education of our children critical? Very.
>
> Do a majority of teachers care about students' wellbeing? I think so.
>
> Can you change the course of the entire system of education in this country at the federal, state, and local levels where the problems and blockers to success are? Ha!
>
> **Whatever your reason is for thinking of leaving,** *it's good enough.*

You are not failing students by leaving.

Society is failing students by disrespecting such a [supposedly] critical position.

And if you are thinking of leaving, this book will help you create a plan. Like any good thing that comes in life, planning and hard work pay off. So, earn it.

notes

In this book I will outline topics like

- Choosing a new career,
- Finding what companies are a good fit,
- Selecting the next job/role,
- Understanding how teaching skills translate to corporate settings,
- Selling your qualifications and telling your story, and
- Reaching out and setting your resume up for success.

And the most important lesson of all? **The power of NETWORKING.**

Throughout this book, I hope to guide you to tell your story so someone takes a chance on you.

And yes, you just might miss out on **that annual *FREE Burrito!!!*** during Teacher Appreciation Week. But I can tell you right now, between finally making enough money to *BUY* said burrito coupled with the ability to go to the bathroom whenever you want?

It. Is. Awesome.

Now What?

FIRST:

Document your values any way you see fit. What is it in life you care about? Who do you care about? Why do you care? Include social, career, family, and self.

I'll say too, I love this. This is not a unique piece of advice. I have been the recipient of this challenge and although I give this advice to teachers who want to change careers, I forget it myself. There have been times in my post-teacher career when I was considering a new company, role, or promotion. Someone I respect very much asked me this very question when I was contemplating pursuing a new role. I wasn't sure if I wanted it. She told me to list my values. If the job was aligned to my priority values, go for it. If not, pass.

My Values

Social:

Career:

Family:

Self:

NEXT: LET'S NOTE YOUR EXPERIENCES.

Suggestion: use a SWOT analysis.

This is a fairly common tool used in corporate strategy planning and as a sales tool.

1. List out **strengths**.
    a. Write where you excel and achieve.
    b. How do you know these are strengths? Give concrete examples.
    c. Examples: Family first, leader, communicator, etc.

2. List out **weaknesses**.
    a. Where are you not so strong? Why? Do you lack the skill or the confidence?
    b. We say "weakness", but it's not weak, it just needs time and attention. These areas need a good gym session, if you will. Spending time here, you'll get stronger.
    c. Examples: Speaking up, saying no when I'm not interested, staying on budget, etc.

3. List out areas of growth **opportunities**.
    a. Put down what you couldn't list as a strength, meaning you haven't excelled or achieved, but you know you can.
    b. These can also be interests and areas you suspect you'd like because you care.
    c. Examples: Going green/a healthy environment, new tech/new software, etc.

4. List where you didn't quite get the outcome you wanted and why (we'll call these **threats**).
    a. In business this is where you'd list competitors or companies that do the same thing or sell the same product. For you, these are items that have kept you from success, held you back in achievement.
    b. Examples: Money, time, family needs out of your control, etc.

Strengths	Weaknesses

Opportunities	Threats

THEN:

Write a statement of what you want and the life you want to live, including a career to support that life. You may not have all the career answers you think you need here, but this is bigger than a job, bigger than your profession. This is more about determining the life you want to live so that you choose a next job, and beyond that, a right career fit.

Want a comfortable or familiar tool? Write the statement as a SMART goal if you'd like.

If I had been prompted to do this for myself 10 years ago? Mine would have been something like this:

I want a new career that challenges me and gives me space to build upon my passion for helping others learn and succeed but also helps me get out of debt and support myself financially. I want this change as soon as possible, before the start of the next school year. I'll know I'm successful in my personal life when my bank account stays in the black, I have savings, and I'm not dealing with sadness and anxiety on Sunday nights before work starts on Monday. I'll know I'm successful in my new career when I earn a promotion and stay longer than two years.

S - Specific
M - Measurable
A - Achievable
R - Relevant
T - Time-Based

The life I want:

BONUS EXERCISE!

For those who are still unsure about leaving, do a simple pros/cons list. I've added a few considerations but be sure to include what matters to you.

	If I stay in teaching	If I choose new career
Impact on finances, retirement		
My personal relationships (with spouse, children, friends)		
Impact on vacation, free time		
My mental health and my happiness		
My passion for helping others, teaching others		

3

My Journey Out and The Lessons I Want to Share with You

This chapter has a lot in it. I'm going to start with my story and tell you how I got out of teaching. But I'm not going to stop there. I'm going to tell you about all of my jobs since leaving teaching. And it was turbulent. I had no guide, no advice, no mentor, no coach. I'm sharing these truths and harsh lessons with you so you can avoid them. You can think of the first three companies as steppingstone jobs. Because of what I learned and the experience they brought me, these were roles that made every job since an advancement. Think about your non-teacher social group today. I bet many, if not most, don't have the same job they got right out of college, nor are they even at the same company. It's normal to have one or two. It took me three to find my path.

But make no mistake, I'd redo every bit of this journey again, exactly how it played out if it meant the career path I have today. Even the worst parts of my corporate job have been better than the classroom.

A quick reminder to refer often to the Glossary in the back of the book; there will be unfamiliar words in this chapter: we're progressing to the corporate world now.

And since good things take time, you can't expect a quick exit. You will need to plan. As my father has always reminded me:

The best time to find a job is when you have a job.

In the next chapter we'll talk about what steps you could/should be taking while you are still teaching in hopes that you can avoid learning the hard way. Like I did.

notes

Getting That First Non-Classroom Job

I got my first non-teaching job because of a Facebook comment I made. See? Told you it was easy.

I kid, I kid. I was lucky as all heck.

I got my opportunity when an acquaintance, another former teacher, posted to Facebook he was headed to Hawaii for work. I made a comment that I too wished I could be going to Hawaii for work. And then I got his DM.

He hadn't thought of me and didn't know I wanted to leave teaching, but of course I could help him. He needed an LMS (Learning Management System) manager and recalled my work with Moodle when we were colleagues. The job was mine if I wanted it, but I had to move out to the Bay Area, California. Well, duh! Of course I'm in.

This was in the spring. I was hoping to move during the summer. Nuh-uh. Not how the corporate world works. He had to get the job requisition approved by leadership and the board. They had to triple check my salary was in the budget and that the business need was really there. They still needed to sign a new license agreement with the LMS vendor. All kinds of things.

> **From that first comment in early spring to the actual offer took more than 6 months.**

So, in May, I begrudgingly signed my contract for the next school year, worked a crap job at a bar that summer because I had no money, and pretty much hated my life. I was pretty low. I know what it's like to want something so bad—to do everything you know how to do to make it happen—and have nothing come your way.

The six months in between the highest high, thinking THERE IS A JOB FOR ME!!! To the anxious, seemingly endless delays that were painting a picture of hopelessness AND the grind of job hunting were the hardest of my life. Everyone goes through rough spots. I'm sure you can relate in some way. Leaving teaching was only one piece of the puzzle. At that time, I was:

- 29 years old and feeling the pressure of "success" by 30,
- Very recently divorced and so sad even though it was the right decision,
- Living in a new town,

notes

- Left with $30,000+ in debt I didn't ask for,
- Living with my parents,
- Struggling with a bank account constantly in the red,
- Living with no savings and no safety net,
- Disowned by "friends" because of the divorce,
- Spending time with people who did not deserve it,
- Spending time with people who were not good for me,
- Stuck in a job I hated,
- Drinking too much,
- Ignoring my grief over an ectopic pregnancy,
- Trying to ignore years of infertility strife on my mental and physical state, and
- Having actual panic attacks for the first time in my life.

What really sums it up was that I ignored my physical, emotional, and mental health completely.

I cried a lot.

And I'll insert here that changing my career didn't fix everything. Counseling did most of the real work, but changing my job helped immensely. Think about it. Our work time takes up an incredible amount of our day, our week, our lives.

A standard workweek is 40 hours. In my case I was teaching full time plus coaching three sports with daily after-school practice or games as well as Saturday practice or tournaments. This made for a 60-hour+ work week. Add my commute to the school, drive to the middle school where I coached and then back home, I was driving more than 160 miles a day round trip. That's several more hours added to my already exhausting day.

And the few days in between sports seasons? I passed out on the couch by 4 p.m. Some days I slept on the couch until I shuffled, half asleep, to my bed at 8:30 p.m.

I applied to EVERYTHING I could find. I was desperate. My resume sucked. I was lost. My skills did not resonate with recruiters, if I even got a call or email back at all.

Then my acquaintance called me back. On the third day of the new school year. **HE OFFERED ME THE JOB!!!!** I was shaken, elated, and of course I said yes to the offer! I'll never forget the pounding in my chest. I could feel the combo of trepidation and adrenaline coursing through my veins. I felt hot and flushed.

notes

Then I called my mom like I always do when I feel out of control and asked her what I should do. She simply said I had better go tell the principal and resign. Wise, wise woman :) She made it seem so easy, so possible.

So I did.

I resigned on the third day of school. And I was terrified. But if you've ever met me, I can take up some space and I am a firm believer in faking it 'til you make it. Confidence goes a long way. It has worked for men decades before women were allowed to enter the conversation.

My neck may get splotchy and red. My cheeks flush, turn pink. I might shake a little bit. My voice might crack or waver. BUT COME AT ME, BRO.

The principal tried to make me feel guilty.

> **What was he supposed to do now?** Try treating your teachers better.
>
> **He worked hard to get me to his campus.** Ugh, well, this campus sucks too.
>
> **Who was going to teach the kids?** Um, you? You're certified. Enjoy.

The district made its threats.

> **The state will revoke my teaching license.** Here, take it.
>
> **Where am I moving to?** That is none of your business.
>
> **What job am I taking?** Pft. Not telling you, but it's not a crappy teaching job, that's for sure!

A few days later, I packed a suitcase. Shipped some bedding. Cried through security. Boarded the plane.

Experiencing My First Non-Classroom Job

About that first job managing the LMS? It was incredible. I had never worked harder in my life—in a good way and a bad way. At times it felt like I was on 24/7 but I was okay with the hustle. For the first time in my professional life, I felt like my work mattered in a way that created forward progress. Teaching a kick-butt lesson still left me feeling stagnant. This felt fast and crazy cool. If I put in extra hours to release the training on a new product that our field personnel could install, that would be money for the company. Helping the company make money meant a bonus for me. I craved that monetary reinforcement. I was tired of being flat broke, in the red, living paycheck to paycheck.

My jaw dropped one day in early December. My boss WAS GIVING ME A BONUS and I had been with the company for LESS THAN FOUR MONTHS. Who just gives out $4,000.00 like that? Companies. That's who.

I worked from Mexico. I worked from my parents' house. I went to Italy with only a moment's notice (pause here for the plug and appreciation that I could *afford* plane tickets to all those places!). I [for the most part] chose when and which office I worked from, or if I even went in at all. For the amazing feeling this brought me, you'll have to think back to pre-COVID pandemic in 2020 when all the world went remote for a minute. This was a time when almost everyone I knew went to an office. Everyone had a set schedule and had to be at their place of employment. Going from a rigid daily, repetitive classroom schedule to flex work? There was nothing like it.

On the flip side, I got sick more in my first tech job than I did teaching 150 high schoolers a semester. I would be up at midnight to test the new SSO (Single Sign On) setup for the LMS I managed. I would be up at 2 a.m. Pacific for 5 a.m. Eastern meetings. If the crew that was going out that day needed help in the LMS, it was me. One time I had strep throat so bad and was insanely dehydrated. The nurse practitioner at the Urgent Care wanted me to go to a hospital. I wanted to get in my Uber and go home. Thank God for Postmates. They brought me my order of Pedialyte and chicken noodle soup.

Working 18-hour days was not healthy. It wasn't healthy when I was teaching and coaching in season. It didn't become any healthier of a situation in tech. But I didn't slow down. I had imposter syndrome so bad. I was scared people would see me at 30 years old and wonder why my skills were lacking. Wonder why I had been out of college for 8 years and needed help navigating the most basic business processes. I certainly felt I had something to prove. Looking back? Those hours were on me. I shouldn't have done it. I could have chosen a better balance, but my drive didn't allow me to.

Another negative is that there was a lot of "tech bro" sh!t I hated. Lots of oddities as to who acted in certain ways and what ramifications did and, let's be honest, DIDN'T come to them.

Would you like an example? Glad you asked, but no. Those stories are not for this book and are a distraction, but it was/is real and that needs to be said. I can't say it was much different than the men at one of the campuses I taught at. Remember the story of the male teacher asking about my dating life in front of students? The team lead who then laughed? The principal who ignored it? So similar.

This first company had some toxic tendencies but not the worst. You saw the acquisition of this company in the news. Essentially its valuation was inflated and that's why the courts got involved. That said, the person who gave me MY BIG BREAK was done dirty. It's not my story to tell but what I'll say about myself and what I learned in my career transition is this:

1. I was naive and did NOT see it coming. Office politics are nasty.
2. I realized how cold and ruthless business can be.
3. I did not want this culture at my next job.

I knew that the men in my department didn't make me feel safe. I think these men also made my manager feel unsafe even though he too was a man. A more experienced me might have known how to navigate a conversation about this with him. Another pause to say that I bet the ratio of men to women in my HQ role in the Operations department was 6:1 male to female and that's giving them a lot of grace. One man in particular gave me the creeps. He stood too close, he leered, and was very open about his personal life, drug use, and his intimate relationships. The cherry on top of all that inappropriateness was that he was scheming and undermining my manager behind his back. So were some of the other men who mirrored the guy I just described. They got my manager fired. They told him at an extremely inappropriate time, and it was far from professional.

Suffice it to say, this job came to an end with a layoff weeks after they did my manager wrong. I got zero equity, meaning ALL of my potential stock (real money) evaporated weeks before I was set to vest. Some companies are managed by and full of blood-sucking boards, VCs (Venture Capitalists), and PE (Private Equity) firms.

Was this better than teaching? ABSOLUTELY. Especially since I received a severance package, my bank account started to rebound, flex work was incredible, I was building my resume with great experience, and I started to make amazing networking connections. I gained confidence in myself, and I realized the skills I used to manage the LMS in my classroom were exactly the same as managing it for an entire organization. *I realized I could make it outside of teaching.*

Another perk I learned about? Sabbatical. I didn't get one but for every three years worked, you got three months paid off and your job was GUARANTEED when you came back. And a program I did get to participate in was the Mentorship Program. I was able to get an experienced mentor, he was in the finance department, and I learned an *incredible* amount! Sal was kind, understanding, and loved my story. He taught me the ins and outs of business and how we actually made money and was just an all-around stand-up mentor that helped me navigate those first six months.

What did I wish I knew mattered before taking a job? The immense importance of company culture.

What were my top three transferable teaching skills?

1. **LMS Admin.** Everything I learned volunteering on campus to run the LMS for at-home teen moms, long-term suspension, students seeking early credit through online options, and students in juvenile detention centers could be relayed into managing the LMS for the corporate world: user setup, enrollment, course assignment, feedback/grading, and reporting.
2. **Lessons Plans.** Documenting coursework and ensuring it followed a standard (state curriculum vs. OSHA standard), included applicable and measurable activities, and was at the reading level of the employee was so much like a documented lesson plan.
3. **Communication.** I was the "expert" and trusted! I knew the most about curriculum design, learning styles, and how information should be communicated and consumed. I was like an internal consultant for anyone who wanted to offer training content about their department and what employees needed to know.

Rebounding From a Layoff

So, what happened next? Scared AF but not one to give up after just going through everything I did to get out of teaching, I was not going to tuck tail and head back to Missouri. I leveraged my relationships, and I will forever be grateful to Jack (not his real name). While at my first job, we had begun looking for new LMS software to partner with. At the time, Jack was the leader of this new software. I loved this product. I wanted to buy it and become their customer. It would have been a nimble, more cost-effective upgrade for us. We were ready to partner.

In August, instead of calling to give Jack our verbal commitment, I asked him if he wanted the bad news or the worse news. I ultimately told him that 1) we would not be getting a deal done and 2) I was laid off. Incredibly, he asked when my severance would be up and gave me the name of a talent manager at his company and said she would be calling. I started the Monday after my severance ran out. I know I have not told him how grateful I was for feeling saved.

But the job wasn't all roses. I took the salary they offered me, when I should have been making more, but I didn't know, and I was too desperate and too uninformed to negotiate. I was comparing a Bay Area tech job salary against my Missouri

notes

teacher salary, not taking into account cost of living but more importantly, I didn't understand my worth and the value of the clients I would be managing. In all honesty, I didn't even realize I could negotiate my salary. I thought that was only for CEOs and something dramatic to write into a movie script.

I managed multiple Fortune 500 companies' custom projects. I continued to work crazy hours. I'd wake up at 4 a.m. to take East Coast calls just in time to run to my local Oakland BART station to take calls on the entire 45-minute train ride to South Bay, connecting into Dublin. To still be on calls on the shuttle ride from BART to the office. Many evenings I'd be the last one there. Especially in the beginning. I was handed a freaking mess of accounts, all unhappy. All over hours, which meant all were over budget.

I was exhausted. My burnout expressed itself as anger. *Cringe.*

I had some good co-workers and teammates, but I wasn't always pleasant. Sometimes I knew in the moment, but when your customer has been up your butt for weeks and your pleas for support to your management team are ignored and go unaddressed, it's easy not to care if you're being "nice." Besides, let's not get started on the BS expectation that women need to be nice in the first place. Plenty of men were outright rude to my face in front of many occupied open cubicles for others to see and zero repercussions came to them. Nasty sales reps can get away with a lot for EarNinG tHe ComPaNY mOneY.

After 2 years of being in tech, I was finding my voice and I wanted a raise badly. Moreover, it wasn't simply a want, I earned that sh!t. My business acumen was increasing. And let's not forget, I'm no dummy. If I'm billing well over a million dollars from my clients, the money for me to get $15,000-$20,000.00 more should have been easy, right? Wrong.

I received a phone call a few days before the Christmas holiday. I was headed to dinner and didn't want to talk at that moment, but I took it anyway. I was waiting for this call. It was an offer for a raise...that included no additional resources (meaning people to help manage the workload) and was an insulting $5,000. Now, to a teacher that is a lot of money. To most people, that is a lot of money. But in the Bay Area? That can feel like $20. It's what makes the area so freaking amazing and full of potential but can make the struggle real. For me, though, that $5,000 didn't even put me where I should have been. I said I wanted $20,000. That's because $10,000 would have put me at the level that other people in the industry were making considering the importance of clients and workload. I made my clients happy, managing between 30-50 active projects at a time, all while also supporting new sales efforts and scoping custom work. Leading a team of around

notes

10 direct reports, indirect resources, and vendor relationships. Coaching and driving progress of coders, QA testers, and implementation. $10,000 more was the promotion I deserved because I worked my ass off.

That phone call was it. I was done. I hung up and my anger was white hot. I coasted through the rest of the holiday season and flipped the radio button on LinkedIn that lets recruiters know I welcome conversations because I'm open to exploring new opportunities. (We'll get more into LinkedIn later in Chapter 8 so you can share this signal too.)

Was this better than teaching? YES. I made so many fruitful client connections, built relationships, upped my business acumen to a very high level, and learned a lot about what matters to companies by supporting their top projects using our software. I presented at a conference for the first time, in Las Vegas! I got to experience working for a female leader (statistically, most leaders are still male). I interacted with executives at this job too. I spoke with the CEO and top executives. And that crazy Bay Area commute? It was no sweat compared to the hours behind the wheel and sitting in traffic. Because on the way home? I read books, listened to music, and texted my family. And keep in mind, I only went into the office a few times a week.

Once again, I realized that although the experience was intimidating, it was so worth it. I also learned what a paid furlough was. During the winter holiday/new year, almost the entire company shut down for a paid two-week vacation. Really. NO WORK. (Not calling it winter break where I was really grading finals.) Amazing!!

What did I need to know before taking this job? Negotiation is real, it is important, and you should not be afraid of it. You do not look pushy or demanding. In fact, it's expected and doing it can show experience (even when you don't have much). Moreso now than ever before, salaries are posted with job openings. There are also websites that specialize in sharing salary information and let people anonymously post what they make and the job they do. Check them out!

What were my top three transferable teaching skills?

1. **Relationship Building.** I had to earn my clients' trust quickly and ensure they knew I was on their team and there to help. I needed them to come to me early with a problem rather than let it get out of hand and escalated to senior leaders.
2. **Teaching!** It was my job to ensure the client was comfortable and knew HOW to use the software they were buying. I had to use materials created by the product team to train and translate. Just like I had to help students with

notes

new jargon and vocabulary words, I had to teach my clients the language of the product.
3. **Presentation Skills and Leading Professional Development on Teacher Workdays.** I presented at my first conference during this job. I had to stand up on stage in front of a room of adults, all clients or prospective clients, and teach them about LMS best practices, finding the right LMS, and how to implement an LMS.

When Planning Goes Right

My next job came when a recruiter called me a few weeks later. The recruiter said my background was a great fit. A large part of this role would be training new hires and leading ongoing learning for the sales team. Since I had two years of tech jobs on my resume combined with seven years of teaching and a master's degree in curriculum and instruction, she was pushing me through the process and setting up multiple calls within this new company. The role was $30,000 more in salary at about 60% of the workload. I was salivating.

I wanted this job so badly. So, I created a plan, did whatever they [the new company] asked, put in more effort than ever before for the interview process, and crushed it. I built a portfolio of work, templatized my teaching materials into corporate materials. I role played, I practiced, I thought about what the most compelling stories were that I could share. A specific example of my strategy? For my in-person interview, I had to create a presentation to coach and teach sales reps how to sell an LMS product against a competitor (they didn't tell us which competitor, we had to choose that. Yes, kind of a gotcha, but that's an interview for ya). So, I did research (there are websites that compare software, check them out). I created the best presentation I could, and I definitely used teaching techniques and content methods I learned in my teacher professional development sessions. And I didn't pick the top competitor by volume. I took a risk, but I wanted to stand out. Other people had the same information I did. They had the same interview prep materials from the open job role as I did (it is common for companies to give you material and information and then ask you to apply it in the interview process).

I chose a top competitor based on a *new feature—a new testing/assessment module*. I got the info about this new product feature from the interview materials I just mentioned. I tailored my playbook agåainst beating a specific attribute of the competition. Does this make me a genius? No! We used to strategize and prep at varsity basketball practice on how to beat a team and win by shutting down the offense of the other team's top scorer, not all scoring. Or by crushing them on the boards and rebounding far more than they did rather than focusing on eliminating turnovers. See? You have stories like this too. You are a professional and know more than you realize. But I digress. I picked what I thought no one else would talk about, went deep on the why, and faked confidence when I practiced until I actually felt confident.

In the interview, I was asked specifically why I picked such a small potato competitor. The guy who asked it took me for a fool, I'm sure. But I had a kickass, unique answer. I articulated that the competitor I chose had a testing module that was superior in a big way. I had data that their testing module was downloaded and integrated into another sales tool MORE than the company I was interviewing for. This was huge as I, in my prep, tried but failed to download the app. Do you know why I couldn't download? I didn't PAY. I equated those downloads to dollars. And the testing module was the new feature shared in the interview materials. I showed that this was a rather worthy opponent who was raking in revenue. I got all this data from public websites. I shared the sources. He sat up straighter while I was presenting. It felt incredible.

Of course, yes, fine, there is the chance that their first option said no to the offer or that many others turned down the job. Whatever. I got it and I made the most of what was right in front of me.

It was my first six-figure job.

In 29 months—that's just under 2.5 years—I improved my pay by 167%. 🤑

And now writing this I refuse to give this job any more of my attention. I simply cannot give it space. At three months in, I knew it wasn't for me. At six months I wanted out. But I stayed to get my equity. Here's the rotten part about high tech. Your vested equity is your long-term pay. There is no pension, usually no 401(k) match. It's why you put up with a whole bunch of nonsense. If you leave before you vest, you leave money on the table. Potential money that could increase with time. Equity packages are why high tech justifies paying a lower salary—your equity makes up for it in the long run.

Was this better than teaching? YES. I got out of debt, I took copious amounts of vacation because we had unlimited paid time off, I stayed at a Ritz Carlton for a conference, I worked from wherever in the world I wanted. I went on my first international business trip. I found my great fit career: enablement.

notes

But why was it a failure? I put so much effort into chasing that salary that I gave zero thought and put zero effort into researching the company culture. If I had looked at company reviews online, asked to talk to current employees during the interview process, or paid attention to anything other than money, I would have known this was not the right move.

What were my top three transferable teaching skills?

1. **Documentation.** Sadly, as we know, not all experiences are good ones... and THOSE are the ones you need good notes for. If a student is showing signs of negative behaviors, you jot those down so you can see a pattern and so you can help. And so you have a history of what has transpired from your perspective.
2. **Data and Analysis.** Much like I would compare pre- and post-test scores or formative assessment data to tweak/revisit/accelerate a lesson or unit, I did the same for my sales bootcamps and onboarding for new hires. I used their onboarding scores and real sales performance data to know what I needed to revisit or go over with them again for coaching programs.
3. **Making it fun!** Onboarding can be rather dry. You have to learn the ins and outs of the company and product. I wanted my employee participants to be engaged so instead of a bunch of death-by-PowerPoint and quizzes, I used more engaging activities like a scavenger hunt or questioning a mentor in an interview.

Making a Bold Move—Attending Events

So once again, at that six-month mark, I created a strategy for how to get a next job and this time, one that I would actually like and could see myself staying at. I now deeply understood how crucial company culture was. I went to a ton of cool networking events. The best part? They were free or only charged a few dollars to get in (and that included food and drinks in addition to meeting the right audience of people!). I thought about what made me a great asset and valuable employee for a company. I honed in on my storytelling. **At networking events, I participated.** At these events I met a lot of great folks that expanded my network. I stayed exactly one year and a day at this company, vested my shares, and had a new job lined up for that next Monday.

Squeezing in another quick lesson: sign nothing when you leave. No "last paycheck" is worth the forfeited power and silenced voice a Non-Disclosure Agreement (NDA) binds you to, maybe for life. And get advice from employment lawyers— ones who are good enough and reasonably priced to help you understand the fine print in any document an employer asks you to sign. Don't let the scary parts intimidate you. You have the right to ask for a day (or two) to think it over and talk to your partner or a lawyer, and to research fair pay for negotiation purposes. Honestly you should be doing this for your teaching contracts. The difference? You can't negotiate your teacher contract. You can negotiate terms in your corporate contracts.

I learned a ton at my next job. Elay is the co-founder and CEO of a revenue enablement software company, and you'll hear more about him later. He is generous with his knowledge, he is a foundational leader in the enablement industry, and he invests time in others. It was while I was at this company that I realized my own considerable potential. I also realized I didn't just love enablement and what it stands for, the impact it can have on a company, a sales team, an individual sales rep, I realized *I was good at it*. It's coaching, and coaching is an investment in a person.

I was in a sales role, a Solution Consultant to put a title to it. It was great because I got to meet a lot of people in the market. I was able to take the enablement learnings from my two previous jobs and apply Elay's expertise and skyrocket my knowledge of all aspects of the enablement field. Deeper learning came from my opportunity to meet with CROs and EVP/SVPs of sales and see real-life examples of revenue strategies and GTM (Go-To-Market) initiatives. It came from hearing our clients tell their success stories and how they solved real revenue challenges when speaking at our customer events. I learned to analyze data and turn it into information that provided insights that were actionable. I expanded my network by 25+ people a week with sales calls. People in the role at all levels: entry, senior, mid-level directors, and high-up leaders. People who I had spoken with on calls, who saw me doing my job, who asked me candid questions and needed honest answers about this new solution to fit their company needs. These weren't just social media connections, they were human relationships.

Was this better than teaching? YES! By this point it was not even a question. It was this experience that allowed me to accelerate my career and not only get a "next job," but open the door to move into an executive role, a leadership role with a large team.

What I still wasn't very good at was communication. I didn't do a great job of voicing what I wanted and while reflecting about this, what I realized is that I had hit a ceiling and craved more but didn't know how to express it the way it needed to be expressed.

notes

What were my top three transferable teaching skills?

1. **Sharing Expertise.** Much like a student looks to their teacher for expertise and the "right" answer, clients needed this from me. I was the solution specialist; I was supposed to know. BUT just like I had to be honest with a student and say I don't know, let's look it up, I had to do the same with a client. I had to be vulnerable and say I didn't know but that I would look it up and get back to them. Crystal in Chapter Ten will share this same tip.

2. **Meeting the Audience (Student) Where They Are.** No matter how much I knew, if my client wasn't following along, it was a failed sales call. I needed to ensure I asked clarifying questions, checked for understanding, and spoke in the client's language, instead of using a bunch of internal terms for our product.

3. **Storytelling.** This became huge, not just in my job of telling success stories about the product to clients and prospects, but at networking events to help forward my own career.

Leaning On Recruiters

Lucky for me, another recruiter called. Enter my last role *fOr ThE mAn*. As I write this, I'm hoping this was my last job working for a company before investing in myself and taking enablement, digital transformation, and coaching to market as my own business full time.

My time at this last company? This is where I hit my stride. Never before in my career was I entrusted with so much responsibility, able to earn another life-changing salary and compensation, and given the opportunity to develop into the people-first leader I wanted to be. At this job my voice has weight. My manager is an incredible advocate for me. Dennis trusts me and I him. My team is incredible; at this time, I can't imagine not working with them. No job is perfect, of course there are challenges. And business politics, private money, and leadership churn are still nasty business, annoying, and inescapable. At the end of the day, work is still work.

But is this job better than teaching? A RESOUNDING YES!

What were my top three transferable teaching skills?

1. **Supportive Command of the Situation.** I recall a student had a seizure in my class. It was scary, but I had to put that to the back of my mind and ACT. I had to call for help immediately, evacuate the classroom to limit exposure to the rest of the students, and tend to the student who needed me in their helpless state. That's a lot like leading a team. Many people need things from me all at once. I have to help those who need it immediately, consider my entire team when taking control of a situation, and ensure

my team is getting help from the company when and how they need it. A corporate example is getting someone who just lost a parent an extended bereavement while ensuring the rest of the team had what they needed while this teammate healed.

2. **Teaching Techniques.** I'll write more about specific examples in Chapter Four, but I use many of my classroom "hacks" on adult employees when training, coaching, and relaying information.

3. **Helping Others.** I've been in the corporate world for 10 years and I'm in a good groove. I have extra time and so I give it to others. In the latter years of my teaching, I wasn't scrambling to get the lesson for the next day completed or the test ready for that Friday. Staying for 30 minutes to help in a study hall for those that needed it? Easy. That's like my schedule now. I can get my work done much easier, so I give time I used to have to use educating myself about my roles and products to teachers who want a career change.

In Summation

So, what was the point of that rollercoaster ride through Ashley's career? It's the lessons learned while in the job and how it prepared me for my next step.

Solar Company

- I was replaceable and layoffs aren't personal.
- There will forever be layers of information you are not privy to.
- The company is not your family no matter how much internal marketing wants you to believe it.
- Protect your time; others will not.
- Imposter syndrome is not helpful. Learn to silence that voice and keep doing your best.
- Always be networking and open to career conversations, especially with vendors.
- Save your money; put away as much as you can.

LMS Company

- Determine your value and use it as a guiding principle.
- If you don't know your value, find a group to join and ask them to help you.
- Hustle culture will kill you. Demand a balance from *yourself* and from your employer.
- Take advantage of client connections. They will be fruitful in the future.
- Be prepared to walk away if they say no.

notes

Sales Tool Company

- Strategize to get what you want. Have a plan and follow through.
- If you feel unsafe, the job is NEVER worth it. Leave. Immediately.
- Sign nothing that you do not understand. If you do sign, it better be worth your silence. You have the right to seek expert, legal advice.

Revenue Enablement Company

- Learn to communicate effectively and in a business capacity. It is not necessarily the same communication style as other areas of our lives and relationships.
- Embrace learning and up your business acumen. It will help with communication too.
- Continuously reflect on your career goals.
- Be open to new experiences. Go to networking events. Even if you determine it was not the scene for you, the time was not wasted.
- Find good mentors and industry experts to build relationships with.
- Be appreciative of cool opportunities.

Omnichannel Communications Company

- Growth is almost always uncomfortable. Chase it and embrace it.
- Get along with your direct manager to make good things happen. Learn from them. Be their best teammate. Support them and have their back.
- Find a mentor who will advocate for you, even when you're not in the room.
- If you genuinely enjoy working with the team you are on and those around you, relish it. Recognize it. That vibe is super special and does not always happen. You will miss it when it's gone.
- **Be your own best advocate for your career.**

If you are itching to hear more stories of teachers who have left the classroom, those are available in Chapter Ten. No one is mad if you skip ahead and read them to get the extra bump of motivation you may need before moving on to Chapter Four.

Now What?

A practical answer is to apply this simple strategy: identify what drains your energy and what gives you energy.

Have your list be a mix of personal and professional but keep it task oriented. You can add things you do outside of teaching. For example:

Drains: List what about work is a clear reminder that you are at work because you do not enjoy the task. Include items such as harsh deadlines (such as paying taxes), too much face-to-face engagement (if you're an introvert), documentation, etc.

Energizes: Essentially list what you do at work that doesn't feel like work. Outside of work it may include your joy in helping with Sunday School at church, monitoring/coaching a community activity (leading your daughter's Girl Scout troop, coaching your son's soccer team, working with cadets in Civil Air Patrol), etc.

*I've found it rather difficult to give examples of drain and energize activities because what drains one person may energize another and vice versa!

I still do this activity for myself in my current roles and engagements. If it energizes me, I try to do more of it. Simple enough.

And if it's on the Drain list, I try to delegate it, automate it, or eliminate it. Not always that simple, but I don't stay stagnant, that I can tell you.

List what drains you.	List what energizes you.
• What activities and tasks do you avoid or procrastinate? • What zaps your energy? • What leaves you feeling depleted?	• What gives you energy? • What doesn't even feel like work? • What leaves you feeling fulfilled?

Once you have this list, refer to your Chapter Two values and SWOT analysis.

Let's dissect it all and answer these questions. Take some light notes. This is more of a thought exercise, but documenting your conclusions will be helpful in the next few chapters as we begin to refine the right immediate activities you get involved in, find company fit, and choose the best roles for you.

1. Do you see commonalities in your values and successes compared to your Energize list? What is the same/tightly related?

2. Of your listed opportunities, how do these compare with what energizes you? Are they similar, or can you at least draw a connection?

3. Do the times you were not successful (weaknesses and threats) include many/multiple Drain items?

4. Now prioritize your lists. What rises to the top of each list for Drain and Energize?

| Top Drain Tasks | Top Energize Tasks |

DISCOVERING YOUR FUTURE

4

Don't Say No
(Setting Up Your Future for Success)

Leaving teaching is a delicate dance of timing. And as you already know from your own experiences trying to get your oil changed, visit the dentist, or any other normal human task, the school day does not align with the flexibility of a corporate workday. So, it should come as no surprise that the school year does not align with corporate budgets and big hiring windows (in general, most companies hire in February/March and September/October).

So, while you're still in the classroom, let's start to craft your plan and what you can do right now so you don't feel so stuck.

There is a lot to take in in this chapter, so go slow, take notes in the margin, and circle what you'll need to come back to.

Steps You Can Take to Make a Change While Teaching

If you're serious about a career transition, you will need to be bold. Taking bold action will be a bit easier with a network to lean on, a great story to tell, and smart execution. That's the rest of the chapters. For now, let's start slowly with what you can do while you are still in the classroom.

But first, let's address those threats of nasty fees and fines from the school district.

Have you ever heard of a signing bonus? I bet you have. You hear about them in sports all the time. Or in car commercials; buy the car and get a $1,000 signing bonus!

They exist in jobs too.

It is a monetary amount, paid in a lump sum when you sign an agreement. Just like for your teaching job, you'll sign a documented job offer and that is what triggers Human Resources to start onboarding you. It is the step after they verbally offer you the job and you say "yes!"

So, if you work for a district that as of late, or has always, put in fees or fines for leaving your "teaching post" early, don't let that stop your search or your momentum. If you are offered a role, negotiate a signing bonus as part of your compensation. Ask for an amount that covers the fee for leaving the classroom. I know the threat of charging you three to five thousand dollars seems daunting, but in business, that is a very common amount to give. We teachers just aren't aware of how much cash and resources are available in the corporate world. We are so used to scraping by that our minds are skewed and $5,000 is enough to scare us. It shouldn't.

Another view you can take? Simply do the math of staying in the teacher salary versus your new salary and compensation plan. Most jobs today post a salary range. Will the new pay be more than your teacher salary plus the fine? I bet it will be. It will be more lucrative to leave and pay the fine than to let the threat deter you. Negotiation shouldn't scare you. Learning about it will make you powerful.

A quick story to ease your mind: my first job gave me almost $10,000 to cover the cost of moving, plus a signing bonus. In later jobs, I got anywhere between $4,000 and $10,000 per job. After a while I stopped with the signing bonuses and negotiated for higher performance bonuses (these weren't cash, these were percentages of my higher salaries).

How did these items come up? At my first job they gave it to me because I didn't know to even ask and as you recall the person who hired me knew me and simply did the right thing! Second job and on? I simply asked. I asked the recruiter about bonuses and compensation after it was clear the job was a fit and I was qualified. That usually gave me some answers and then since I had more information, *after* I was offered the job by the hiring manager, I would ask about what else I wanted (more paid time off, signing bonus, performance bonuses, etc.). There's no trick except money shouldn't come up first, it comes up in the end after you've built the relationship. Again, everything is negotiable. Not everything is a yes, but everything can be discussed.

Don't Say No

Yes, this chapter is titled "Don't Say No." "Yes, Please"[1] was already taken (such a good read, BTW).

And if you are reading this, you've probably said or wanted to say "no" to a lot at school in the past year or two…or five. Maybe you had a choice in the matter, maybe you didn't. Or maybe you were willing to say yes to joining a committee but kept getting passed up, so you stopped asking. Or maybe you weren't even asked to join. Your past experiences might give you pause, so I want to be clear about what you are saying yes to. You say yes and pursue a new opportunity if you can tie it to helping you leave the classroom.

Change your approach and mindset. Get a little strategic. Not only is strategy a huge part of the business world (more on this later), but having a strategy to allow you to change careers is vital. Following a path is easier and far more productive than winging it. Taking on more might seem daunting, especially if you're unhappy, but changing your mindset to "this will help me grow" **AND** "this too shall pass" **AND** "this just might be the thing that gets me the heck out of this teaching job" will make the effort worthwhile.

What a luxury to be stress free and go home at the end of the workday, not having a care in the world. In my teaching experience, that was not real life. Definitely not most teachers and certainly not me. How many times as a teacher did I say to myself, "Oh!! This would make such a great lesson!" and take planning work home? How often did I give extra time to helping a kiddo with a job or college application, stay late to listen to a student and be mental/emotional support, or attend a school

---

[1] Poehler, Amy. (2014). *Yes Please*. New York: Dey Street.

performance? Too many to count. And most of my peers were no different; you're no different. Kids time and time again get our time, our passion, and our emotion.

Not to mention, I was a coach after school. I supervised Saturday detention. I managed the online LMS. I was on committees. Granted, some of my "extra" was for stipends, pennies per hour when you break down the time-to-dollars ratio. But most were unpaid.

Today, I still take my work home. I love it. I love the challenge and I love knowing that I make an impact and that others are relying on me to complete my piece of the puzzle, be it my boss, co-worker, or customer. However, when I was a teacher and took work home it just meant that at the end of the week I worked more. Now in my career if we have a big week and I work extra? The next week I am not putting in 40 hours. I'm taking my time back—going to an appointment midday without hesitation, taking a Wednesday afternoon off early, grabbing coffee with a networking connection on a Friday morning.

But for you, currently in the classroom, agreeing to take on more this time can't be about money (but if you can get paid extra, do it) or simply supporting your students as an audience member. The committees, the task forces, the teams you can be part of are usually unpaid and will have the most impact in your career transition, as long as these "yeses" fit into your strategy.

When an opportunity presents itself to be part of something worthwhile, say yes. Don't let the hours the union impresses upon a school district push you to say no and not stay after school. Is the money there? No. Is there even free coffee? Maybe, but probably not. But do it anyway. The dividends pay off later and nothing good, I mean nothing *really good*, gives instant gratification.

Even if you're not interested, say yes. You never know what it may bring.

But wait.

Some things are an easy no because they are not a strategic "yes":

- ⊘ Extra playground duty.
- ⊘ Standing in the pick-up/drop-off car line longer.
- ⊘ More cafeteria duty.
- ⊘ Friday night football game supervision.
- ⊘ Making copies for the lazy teammate.
- ⊘ Cleaning up the breakroom after a luncheon.
- ⊘ Setting up or taking down folding chairs.

notes

Here are some "Don't Say Nos" from my past that have helped me, some of which still help me as I build my own career.

I also want to emphasize that I did not do all of these examples I'm about to tell you about at once. You should not read this and think, "I have to do everything suggested." You don't. Read it all and find what is possible for you and focus on one thing at a time. There is no need to overwhelm yourself.

Programs

I have two really great examples of teaching programs helping me in my non-classroom career.

Classroom Management and Student Relationship Processes

On one of the early campuses I taught at, I had to complete a relationship and classroom management training called "Capturing Kids' Hearts." Some of my colleagues HATED it. It was very touchy-feely and not everyone's cup of tea. But it was what it was. Every teacher had to implement this strategy in their classroom. The difference between me and most of them? I embraced the hell out of it—I had loftier goals. I was all about participation. I hung my Social Contracts on the wall. I asked the four questions to redirect behavior. I actually got really good at it. Later, other teachers would come to my classroom (not by choice—yeesh, super awkward) to watch me get after it. I felt seen in a good way. And it was because of this attitude that I was asked to be part of Part II. I completed the Ambassador program with zeal.

Here's the thing. The program itself is irrelevant. What I realized about this whole situation was that the principal LOVED it. He lived it. It wasn't a classroom initiative to him or a "go through the motions because it is a job requirement and the district is making us" thing. The program aligned to his personal values and how he lived life outside of work. It was about creating meaningful relationships and communication, especially during times of disagreement or conflict. This made it easy for me to go all in, but to be clear, it was his dedication and belief that made this an opportunity to take on a volunteer role that allowed me to grow in leadership and be part of a larger strategy outside my classroom door.

So, if your leadership (principal, lead counselor, a district rep, school board member) is this "all" in on a program, a methodology, and ideology? That's your "yes." That's a reference. That's the opportunity to be part of leadership. This is the opportunity to see how to roll out a program at scale and be part of it. It is a way to

notes

practice good networking. You are in on the strategy if you approach it that way. If you don't know what they care about, find out. Ask them. Then give it your time.

Teaching Techniques

I love the book, *Teach Like a Champion* (TLC). In all honesty, I loved it when the assistant principal rolled it out one morning during our professional development time. It feels natural to pause here and say this was the same campus that rolled out Capturing Kids' Hearts. This was a group of admirable campus leaders. I believe the head principal went into a district leadership role. He should've. He is the kind of leader public education and teachers need. Now, back to the task at hand: joining committees and finding corporate value.

Teach Like a Champion is a list of 49 instruction and communication techniques to help engage students, facilitate learning, and measure student abilities. I still apply my go-to classroom techniques when leading corporate training sessions. I have 20 of the 49 techniques highlighted, bookmarked, and sticky-noted because I used them, and still use them, all the time. Now that I manage a team, I give these tips to my team members to use. They don't always know they are using classroom best practices, but if it works, no need to mention it, right? For those that do know this is from my past, I've mailed them a copy!

Here are the five classroom teaching techniques (in no particular order, summarized in my own words) that have helped me most in the business world. All you need to do is reframe your brain:

Student Growth and Grades—Employee Progress and Outcomes

Classroom Teaching Technique from Teach Like A Champion[2]	Application in the Corporate World
Right is Right *The job of a teacher is to set a high standard for correctness: 100 percent. This means "almost correct" is not good enough.*	When money is on the line—for the business, for the client—get it right. Providing correct answers/data that are clear and concise is required. Accidents happen. Be hyper vigilant to eliminate them and get it right. Positive outcomes for all rely on it.

[2] Lemov, Doug. (2010), *Teach Like A Champion.* San Francisco: Jossey-Bass.

notes

Classroom Teaching Technique from Teach Like A Champion[2]	Application in the Corporate World
Without Apology *Sometimes the way we talk about expectations inadvertently lowers them. If we are not on guard, we can unwittingly apologize for teaching worthy content and even for the students themselves.*	Not everything about work is pleasant. Not all conversations internally or with clients are good news. You may not personally like the company's choice of direction. Change is also hard. You can't go down a path to new or improved if you are undercutting the decision or plan. Trust it, believe in it, support it.
Begin With the End *Frame an objective first, not the activity. An objective is measurable, an activity is a means.*	A lot of waste happens in business because folks are too short-sighted, not strategic enough, or focus on tasks. Know the company objective.
Check for Understanding *Constantly seek opportunities to assess what students know and can do, and how they do it.*	Treat your peers, cross functional teammates, direct reports, indirect reports, vendor partners, and leadership team the same in this regard: constantly check for alignment and that all are working towards the same outcome. Be sure everyone knows the information they need, is taking the agreed-upon action, and that the processes used are what's best for the company and client. Be the catalyst and connector. People will love it.
Warm/Strict *Combine and balance these seemingly (but not) opposite concepts to help students understand that either-or choices are a false construct.*	Talking to a student with a developing mind is not the same as talking with the fully formed mental capacity of an adult. That said, even in business you can keep kindness in mind as you navigate a project or support a client but still hold everyone involved accountable. This goes hand in hand with Check for Understanding.

notes

Again, it's not the program or approach that matters. It's looking at the situation critically and applying what you are doing, or have to do, in the classroom to a larger goal. It can be any book, any technique, any teaching approach.

Task Forces/Committees

Usually campuses, districts, and states have several task forces or committees. Although joining any one of them would be great, there are three focus areas I recommend for transitioning into the business world.

The Technology Committee

If there is one, get on it. Join the waitlist if you have to. Get exceptionally comfortable with software. Be familiar with it all. Read the support articles. Watch the YouTube videos about it. Didn't even know the online gradebook had a support site? Google it. Visit it. Read it. Get comfortable with the jargon and troubleshooting (fixing) small problems on your own.

If the hardware is a challenge—your laptop, iPad, interactive board—figure it out. No excuses. Then focus on the software.

My work with Moodle LMS I mentioned earlier in the book was unpaid. Complete volunteer work. But I could see the opportunity there. Learning about new technologies and delivery methods, and the ability to use them successfully, for multiple reasons, is huge.

Raise your hand to roll out iPads, update the classroom carts of laptops. Install new software on them.

Become your campus expert of these software programs at the peer level. My guess is there is one person on campus who gets a paid stipend to do this. Maybe it fell into the librarian's lap? So what? Business is competitive and you need tech chops to transition into ANY business role.

Sacrifice your lunch hour once a month or once a quarter. Host a Lunch-N-Learn to teach interested peers the hacks, tips, and tricks you learned from putting in the work. Start a teacher community and meet voluntarily after school, before school, or at lunch. Just get together and get comfortable with tech/software. It doesn't have to be an hour-long ordeal. You can meet for 15-20 quality minutes. Time is not the decider of value here. The content is.

Unsure if anyone would join you? ASK and remember: if you build it, they will come.

Assessment Committees and Curriculum Committees

Business is all about outcomes. The most desired outcome is revenue. Successful businesses understand this and work extremely hard to achieve high revenue, keep it, and adjust to a constantly changing market. Unsuccessful businesses understand this too but somewhere along the way fumble in their strategy, planning, or execution.

The best way to practice these skills is to join assessment or curriculum committees. I joined several while still teaching and looking to leave. Not because I knew it would work, but mostly out of desperation to expand what I could say I was a part of. Even before I knew I wanted to leave teaching I was constantly searching for new challenges outside of my classroom course schedule.

Why spend your precious time on assessment writing and curriculum design committees? You can learn how to:

- Practice alignment from state to district to campus.
- Keep your audience in mind when designing a flow of information intake.
- Focus on how knowledge will be measured.
- Take into consideration multiple learning styles and preferences.
- Write assessment questions for all levels of knowledge measurement.
- Use verbs in design to link knowledge to action.
- Create instructor guides and companions to deliver information.
- Understand formative and summative assessments regarding learner abilities.
- Apply best practices when creating content and lessons, such as Backward Design.
- Map all lessons, content, and assessments to a larger standard.
- Design with outcomes in mind: passing, milestones, etc.
- Anticipate and design remediation and additional coaching for students who need it.
- Make content flexible and modular to meet many campus schedule needs.
- Facetime with state- and district-level leaders.
- Collaborate with peers also on the committee.
- Communicate deeper with peers in addition to parent communications.
- Integrate technology and digital transformation into the new assessments and curriculum.

notes

- Create your own opportunities to lead professional development due to this experience.

You'll want to mark this page for when completing the activities in Chapter Six. You'll learn to say these skills but in corporate speak and align these skills to jobs.

Here (creating and thinking in assessment and curriculum terms) is where as a teacher you can really shine in business; you simply need to change the language you are speaking.

Let's break this down:

I realize that some (maybe almost all!) in the Business column may be unfamiliar to you. Here is my suggestion. Circle what you need to come back to. Jot your questions in the margin and take notes. In Chapters Five and Six we'll discuss good-fit companies and careers for you. Come back to this chart after you research and find companies and jobs you like. Then, using the content on their website and job postings, come back and connect the dots between your teaching skills and what you've found in your research.

In Education	In Business
State Standards	**Key Performance Indicators (KPIs)**
Every state has learning standards. These are areas that all students must demonstrate some sort of proficiency in.	Companies need to be able to measure employee success using behaviors that tell if revenue targets will be met.
They have several layers to them (I'm talking DOK: Depth of Knowledge).	They have several layers to them. Some are Know, some Say (explain), some Do (act).
Some are facts and recognition. Others are verb driven and an action or skill a student needs to execute and apply.	Some are easier, such as knowing how or why a solution will help a customer. Some are difficult, such as demonstrating a solution.
There is no wiggle room. They are what they are whether you as the teacher like them or not.	There should be very little wiggle room. Every KPI should tie back to the company revenue and success plan for that year.
They are measurable. You can benchmark them, show change.	They are measurable. You can benchmark them, show change.
Student performance on them impacts revenue the district can be awarded.	Employee performance of them impacts revenue the company can be awarded.

notes

In Education	In Business
Lesson Plans	**Project Management**
Lessons make up the curriculum.	Tasks make up a project plan.
The curriculum is based on state standards.	Project plans are based on company strategy.
Often a curriculum is mapped to state standards to ensure students can stay on track, it flows.	Often projects are mapped back to company KPIs so departments and teams stay on track.
Most schools or districts have a recommended template or a checklist of items to include in a lesson plan.	Most companies will have a tool or method they commonly use, but if not, most teams make up a checklist of tasks to include.
Lessons have measurable aspects and are checked in along the way and usually have a final assessment to be graded.	Project plans have milestones and target completion dates along the way and a final due date with performance measurement.
Formative Assessment	**1:1 Coaching with A Manager**
Tie back to the state standard.	Discussions about job tasks, career goals.
Steps along the way to earn a passing grade.	Meetings to support personal growth.
Checks for understanding along the way.	Touchpoints to support the employee.
Students can demonstrate their understanding of the material.	Employees can express where they need help, concerns, or desires to progress.
These are not about passing, yet.	These are not performance reviews, yet.
Most of these "grades" don't even go in a grade book.	Most of these meetings go undocumented and very informal but have a loose agenda.
These are for practice and staying on track.	They are for communication, staying on track.
Teachers should be honest in their feedback about student progress and partner with the student to make a plan to achieve success.	Managers should be honest in their feedback about employee performance and partner with the employee to plan for a promotion.

notes

In Education	In Business
Summative Assessments/Grades	**Competencies/Skills Matrix**
Tie back to the state standard.	Tie back to job roles and company KPIs.
A culminating measurement of a student's demonstrated grasp on the state standard(s) required to pass the course.	The measurement of an employee's demonstrated grasp of the skill(s) required for their role.
Sometimes these measure a unit, theme, or entire curriculum.	Competencies can measure all aspects of a role at multiple levels—know, say, and do.
Failing or not passing usually results in required extra practice, study hall, or tutoring.	Performing below the necessary benchmark usually results in additional coaching/training.
Succeeding or passing usually has a positive outcome.	Succeeding or passing can mean a promotion.
To measure, teachers use keys or rubrics to maintain consistency between all students.	To measure, companies can use a variety of methods, and it can feel like a gotcha if not communicated clearly. Not all roles will/should require the same level of mastery.
Rubrics include various levels of achievement or identify where progress is needed.	
At times those keys and rubrics are adjusted to meet the student at their level and making tweaks to help is good practice.	Companies who hire folks not at the required level now owe it to that employee to grow them and tweak the onboarding path.
How scoring and measurement is occurring should be clear to the teacher, student, and parent.	How progression and growth tracking is occurring should be clear to the trainer, employee, and manager.
Team leads, vice principals, or principals own the accountability to ensure measurement is occurring at the required cadence.	Front line managers, people leaders, and executive sponsors own the accountability to ensure measurement is occurring at the required cadence.
At times district personnel or principals may sit in the classroom to observe assessments.	At times training coaches or managers may sit in the meetings or simulations.

notes

In Education	In Business
Parent-Teacher Conferences	**Performance Reviews**
The goal of the meeting is to track performance.	The goal of the meeting is to track performance.
Thoughtful preparation is required.	Thoughtful preparation is required.
The student should participate and own parts of the discussion.	The employee should own the meeting and, at minimum, participate.
Participants should discuss areas of interest and strengths of the student as well as identified areas of needed growth and opportunity.	Participants should discuss areas of interest and strengths of the employee as well as identified areas of needed growth and opportunity.
Student performance should be explained and aligned to the state standards and rubrics.	Employee performance should be explained and aligned to the company KPIs and role competencies.
Decisions should be made: require remediation for additional support or add extracurricular/free time for exploration and higher order thinking.	Decisions should be made: require remediation for additional support or participate in company programs for career growth and promotion.
Daily Instruction	**Status Meetings**
Lessons tie back to the state standards.	Check-ins that tie back to the KPI/goal.
Time allotted to engage with learning.	Steps along the way to achieve the target.
Include Q&A and knowledge checks.	Checks for progress and alignment.
Students can practice skills and grow knowledge to progress their learning further.	Employees can show how their tasks have progressed the group further to completion.
Scheduled, with a routine, interactive.	Scheduled, an agenda, formal or informal.
Led by the teacher. Participation from students.	Led by the project lead/owner. Participation by other employees with assigned tasks.
These lead to a summative assessment.	These track to the final launch or rollout.
Most of these classes are not attended by the principal or vice principal.	Most of these meetings are not attended by leadership.
Ensure progression of the curriculum.	These are for alignment and staying on track.

Don't Say No (Setting Up Your Future For Success)

notes

Leadership Roles

I want to start with some alignment here so you know where I'm coming from:

> **Leadership is not the principal and vice principal.**
> **Leadership is not a title.**

There is *so much more* that encompasses what true leadership is: as a trait, as a practice, as what you can accomplish simply by stepping up, aligning resources, and owning something.

Sadly, from what I hear from teachers, there aren't any opportunities for leadership on their campus. Wrong. By title, that may be so. There are only so many principal, vice principal, and lead counselor roles available in any given school district, on any given campus. But cultivating your leadership abilities creates opportunities for yourself beyond teaching. A core belief of mine:

> **You can lead from any seat.**

Increasing your ability to share with a recruiter a leadership success story and documentation of successful outcomes due to your leadership on your resume is needed to make a transition out of teaching. Do this sooner rather than later. Stop waiting for I'm-Not-Even-Sure-Who to invite you and just start doing.

What do these leadership opportunities look like?

You read above to join the formal committee. If you've already taken that first step and joined, congratulations. Now, push yourself:

- Is the committee leadership spot up for grabs? Apply for it. If it's filled or you weren't selected, go talk to the leader.
- Are they happy? Do they even want it? Take away their burden and turn it into your opportunity. Chances are they will be grateful to offload something they don't want.
- If they are happy in the role, ask what portion of the committee you can own. Can you take on a special project? Can you lead a division or small task force? If you ask and are willing to put in the effort, chances are, there is something you can lead, own, and impact.

People don't usually turn down offers of help.

I'm serious when I suggest that you start your own mini community/task force. Especially if all the committee leadership and chair positions are full.

- Consider an area of need on your campus.
- Get a few like-minded individuals on campus.
- Meet. Plan how you would like to solve this problem.
- Be clear as to what improvement and impact this will have.
- Gather benchmark/starting point data and measure as you go.
- Create a detailed, thoughtful plan.
- Put time, milestones, and outcomes in the plan.
- Consider the budget (extra money in education is laughable but consider if you can).
- Make it clear where and when the anticipated improvement will be due from this work.
- Schedule time with the campus leadership and get buy-in.

Voila! Be a leader of a committee/task force AND improve where you work.

Take the same strategy from above and apply it to other campuses. Can you bring this to other campus principals? District reps or the board? Can you use the same approach to solve a different problem?

In business, if your boss has to micromanage you and constantly dictate your daily activities, no one will be happy. However, if you see a need, take the initiative, keep the boss informed, and make an improvement without being told? That is how you grow from entry-level to higher-level roles with more responsibility, opportunities, and compensation.

Speaking Engagements

Public speaking is still a top fear of a majority of people. I'm sure in some ways it always will be. With so much online engagement and lasting impact of how we lack in-person situations due to the pandemic, we may even see trends over time where the fear grows. However, being a great public speaker is such an amazing tool to have in your toolkit. And teachers straight up have an advantage. **Hear me when I say, as a teacher, you are better than most.** You speak to rooms full of parents and students all the time. You have more "at bats" and practice with this than almost anyone else competing for that corporate job you are applying for.

notes

Even if you have not had the opportunity to speak at a conference or during professional development, I'm sure you've listened and been an audience member. Think about the best presentation sessions you have been part of. In the corporate world there is a lot to compete with in regard to attention. Start to compile what tactics and experiences were the best and craft how you would speak and deliver this content to a non-school-aged audience. Note what was most effective when you were an audience member and keep that for yourself for when you do get an opportunity to present to adults, not students (hello, interviews and interview panels).

If you don't have "good" examples, go find brands you like and find their content online. Almost all companies have webinars and marketing out there. Here's an example: on your campus you most likely have attendance software. Go to that website. You should be able to see the type of content they are training your district and campus IT department with. You'll find presentations, case studies, and webinars you can watch. Whether it's new features, product releases, or training on how to up adoption of the software, these will be great examples of the types of internal presentations given in a corporate, market setting. Actually, these will be better because they are public. The quality of the internal material at most places is much lower (Seriously, don't let imposter syndrome get to you. The bar is far lower than you can imagine in some places). Strong presentations to adults are attainable for you.

I focus on discussing public speaking here because I believe that approaching engagements in the business world will be more fruitful and help you stand out more if you invest in improving your public speaking to adults rather than teenagers, tweens, and children. You'll need this skill to tell your story at networking events, to recruiters or hiring managers, and in interviews.

Where can you get some "at bats"?

- Demonstrate any software or strategy to other teachers at a team or department meeting.
- Present at a conference. Don't let the lack of opportunity provided by your school district stop you. Apply on your own, especially to events that are local and within driving distance. If you get the opportunity to show up and present, take PTO and go!
- Present at campus professional development days. What can you present about? Pick a solution you are implementing and report on the successes and adjustments you've made along the way (all the more reason to join a committee, be a program ambassador, or start your own task force).

- District professional development days. Same suggestion as campus PD time.
- Present at parent-teacher conferences or open houses on a topic your principal needs shared with attendees.
- Partner with the campus instructional coach and work together on a presentation and deliver it to whomever is the intended audience (principals, teachers, or parents).

Get Scrappy

At my very first job out of college, I was not a classroom teacher but rather an even lower paid- (but still paying into teacher retirement) study hall monitor. I had to be certified to be paid this poorly. Yuck. I did still get the same planning time as the other teachers, but sitting on your hump for two hours a day gets monotonous really quick. Plus, it was hourly work and I didn't get paid for that "planning" time, I just had to be there, on campus. Makes total sense to no one.

Instead of wasting this time, especially since it was unpaid and I was fully certified, I raised my hand to be a sub in the social studies department. This way I could teach the class and the district assigned sub could cover my study hall. It gave me tons of face time with students and the other teachers. Because the classroom teacher knew and trusted that I could teach a lesson, they didn't lose an instruction day. I got some good advice and mentoring from the other teachers too.

It was in this same role that I offered up my free period to the department. The department head approved me to function as a teacher assistant for an assigned classroom teacher and we did essentially another semester of student teaching. I did the bulk of the work for the experience and she got time back. It was a win-win for both of us.

If you're young in your career, this is exactly the type of offer you can be making to your campus to get more exposure and practice where you want (act as the teacher assistant for the business or technology teacher once a week on your planning period, anyone?).

Now What?

It doesn't really matter how much or what you take on. What matters is you see how and what opportunities align to your next step of growth and pursue them. Execute them with the mindset that this work can teach you something and build skills you will need in the business world.

Some of you are lucky and thinking, I'm already a part of something. Awesome! Apply what you are already doing to the following activity.

If you're someone that needs to join or start your own, cool. Find the opportunity, then GO DO.

First, compile a list of opportunities to grow and lead while still a teacher.

Later, once you've read and completed the research in Chapters 5 and 6, come back and turn it into corporate-friendly language.

"Don't Say No" Activities I Can Start Today or Pursue	How This Will Help Me in My Corporate Role

Next, reflect on the Chapter Two and Chapter Three activities. From your list above:

★ Star what maps best to your values and strengths and gives you energy.

⊘ Cross out or remove ideas based on what you DON'T want to pursue (Drain list).

Then, get started:

1. Want to join an existing committee? Go talk to the current leader.
2. If currently on a committee, ask to lead a project or chair position.
3. If starting your own, email colleagues or talk to others you think would be interested in joining you to make a difference.

BONUS EXERCISE:

Make a list of transferable skills. To start, we are only going to focus on your classroom teaching skills. You'll make this harder on yourself than it needs to be if you add the pressure to make these into corporate speak. You'll do that after reading the next chapter.

Identify your top five classroom and teaching skills and techniques.

ONE

Skill or technique:

Why I excel at it:

What successes or positive outcomes do I see, do parents see, do students experience?

Real life example:

TWO

Skill or technique:

Why I excel at it:

What successes or positive outcomes do I see, do parents see, do students experience?

Real life example:

THREE

Skill or technique:

Why I excel at it:

What successes or positive outcomes do I see, do parents see, do students experience?

Real life example:

FOUR

Skill or technique:

Why I excel at it:

What successes or positive outcomes do I see, do parents see, do students experience?

Real life example:

FIVE

Skill or technique:

Why I excel at it:

What successes or positive outcomes do I see, do parents see, do students experience?

Real life example:

5

Develop a Growth Mindset and Find What Fits You

Most of you reading this are currently in the classroom pondering how you can make a change. Maybe you're desperate for it to happen quickly or your internal dialogue is whispering that teaching might not be for you in the long run. Or you're the person married to, living with, a friend of, or related to a teacher who you feel needs a change (because you cannot continue to hear the complaining?) and you want to help. Whether you're the teacher or teacher adjacent, you most likely have a good idea where you/your loved one falls on a spectrum of career change readiness.

What makes this leap to leave so difficult for teachers?

We are used to being experts.

notes

We are hyper organized, and not only do we embrace process to an extreme level, we very much fear deviation from it. Yes, we say we are flexible, but every teacher is disgusted with the constant interruptions: pep rallies, academic meetings, field trips, testing, changing lunch shifts, constant bad behavior from the same student, yearbook pictures, early releases…

Bigger ticket items? New grade methodology, tweaked curriculum, new lesson plan template (why spend time shuffling the same deck?), changing your classroom location, passing you from grade to grade or flipping you from Algebra I to Geometry, adding four new students in October…

Couple our natural tendencies with the fact that our entire career plan and path is tightly mapped out with thresholds of required performance and labels and certifications.

- It starts with cadet teaching and being latchkey "teachers" in high school.
- Then we observe classrooms during sophomore year of college.
- A few more credits and we begin student teaching.
- Then we are summer school aides or camp counselors in the summer.
- Then we graduate college, a major in teaching, minor in a subject area.
- We take the state assessment, get the required score to pass, become certified.
- We know what additional tests are for what subjects.
- We know the required number of annual professional development hours.

Once we are on the job?

- The curriculum is dictated to us; Common Core or whatever those who don't actually teach have told teachers what to teach.
- We must document our lesson plans just so. (I Can…stay sane this school year?)
- We struggle to understand for ourselves, much less explain to students and parents, the 1-2-3 assessment method or graduated grade scale.
- We are told exactly how to log attendance and given a submission deadline within a few minutes of the start of class.

- We are told exactly when we must be on campus in the mornings.
- We know down to the minute when we can leave for the day.
- We are told when we can have a break.
- We are told we cannot leave the classroom, bathroom breaks included.
- We are told we have to pay $1 to wear jeans.

And even more important?

- We know our entire pay scale for our entire careers on Day 1 of employment.
- We know there are only two ways to advance: years tick by or pay for Masters, then Doctorate credit hours. A small bump at 15 hours halfway mark, a few more dollars at supplemental degree earned.
- We have three options: stay in the classroom, become a principal, or become a counselor.

Does that sound flexible to you? Heck no. It is a path planned to the extreme. Bucking that amount of certainty is **S C A R Y**.

I have self-service videos that accompany this guidebook and activity items within it. These next chapters are all meant to get you into a good-fit job and build upon it your new career. Check out the additional help to ease your transition and silence your self-doubt.

I know what you're thinking to yourself right now. Probably along the lines of:

> "If I'm not a teacher, what am I?"

Yes, we tell our kiddos "there are no dumb questions" and beg our straggler students to ask for help. We tell students to "go look it up" if they don't have an answer. We provide extra study materials and guides to befuddled parents. We tell students to join a study group or have a study buddy. We chop up eight tired worksheets to make one great reference for our learners. We read the book. We take the notes. We raise our hands. We engage.

We tell our students that with the right preparation, they can go just about anywhere for trade certification, university or college. We tell them they can also go right into the workforce. The military. The family business. Travel, see the world. We tell our students they can follow whatever path they design, work for, and pursue.

Develop a Growth Mindset and Find What Fits You

notes

But for some unfortunate reason this stops when it comes to listening to our own advice.

Why do we not ask for help? Design a new path? Be anything we want when we grow up?

Why don't we Google it when we don't know?

Why don't we hear ourselves when we say design your own future? Make a change?

Fear. Ego. Ignorance. Probably a lot of reasons, none of them good enough not to get started.

If you want to make the change, you need to:

- First, develop a growth mindset and calm your fears.
- Second, educate yourself by researching companies and industries that align to your values and interests.
- Third, get comfortable with data and measurement.

First, to remove fear, do exactly what you'd tell your students:

- Dream big.
- Design your own path.
- Look up what you don't know.
- Create a plan.
- Assign time frames.
- Follow your plan.
- Measure your progress.
- If it's working, keep going.
- If not, adjust.

If you've read the above and still think you're a bit stuck, I suggest pausing here and read up on Carol Dweck's "Growth Mindset."[3] Reading her entire book would be a great spend of time, but what has helped me most in my transition is keeping in mind these snippets of her wisdom:

- Hard work, effort, and determination will outperform and get you further than natural intelligence or being "smart."

---

3 Dweck, Carol S. (2016). *Mindset: the new psychology of success.* New York: Ballantine Books.

- Believing you can, planning, and taking action will move your life in the direction you desire (growth mindset).
- Believing you cannot, that you are not smart enough, or that your skill set is stagnant and unable to improve will hinder meeting life goals, success (fixed mindset).
- Learn from mistakes. Let failure be a teacher.
- Silence the negative thoughts and reframe situations in a positive way.

By choosing to have a growth mindset, you begin to use fear and failure differently. They become teachers with lessons to learn. Adopting a growth mindset helps create comfort in the unknown. Familiarity with how you react to, and address, change can eliminate risk. Eliminating risk is what will make change seem more attainable and less frightening. Failure won't impede your growth; you'll find it becomes a catalyst of success. Hearing 'no' a lot is fine; you only need one 'yes.'

— ◎ —

Second, expand your knowledge and understanding of how businesses work and what solutions they offer. Start by thinking about, then researching, companies you like, those that mirror your values and interests.

But, before you start Googling, I want to address the all-important topic of company culture. Like I've told you before, I messed up when it came to evaluating culture. Let's make sure you keep it top of mind as you begin your research.

Company performance is impacted by many factors, their plan to make money only being one.

There is a saying I heard at my second job after leaving teaching. Since that job I've heard it many more times at the next companies I joined, at conferences during presentations, and in conversations. And it's no wonder. The famous quote is from esteemed business and management consultant Peter Drucker:

"Culture eats strategy for breakfast."

notes

In the previous chapter we discussed how business is all about outcomes, the most desirable being revenue. Again, some companies have a plan to hit their revenue targets and succeed, while others either have a poorly designed plan or don't really have one. 😁 These companies will miss their targets.

All that being said, the plan is only as good as the people. No different than lesson plans. You could have AMAZING activities planned, but if it doesn't align to what's in the curriculum, it won't be reflective of what is in the state exam in which students need certain scores to move on. Students won't perform well, and the district needs high performance to receive state and federal funding. If the lesson plan doesn't engage your students, they won't participate, they won't retain knowledge, and they won't successfully be able to apply skills. Another aspect is how the students feel in your classroom. No, they are not your friends, and it should not be a free-for-all. But the vibe can be chill; the students should know procedures and be trusted to act accordingly, should be empowered to ask questions and own their learning.

When students know they have autonomy and physiological safety, and they have confidence in what is expected of them, they will thrive. *They will perform well, even if the lesson plans **aren't** that great.* This describes employees at a company too.

This is what is meant when you hear "culture eats strategy for breakfast."

A thorough and well-thought-out revenue plan is irrelevant if the employees despise working there.

Here's one of my experiences after I began considering culture for a next role. After riding the high-tech rollercoaster of cool new roles followed by layoffs and acquisitions, permission by omission of nasty behavior, and opportunities to grow and be promoted, I got smart about company culture.

One of my personal checkboxes is DEI (Diversity, Equity, Inclusion) of gender. Yes, plenty of important topics around DEI, but I don't want to distract, and a focused conversation is deserved, not a quick gloss over. In my experience what I realized I needed to look out for is how many females were in leadership positions.

One of the recruiters I'd worked with in finding a next role presented me with a very cool opportunity. It was a good growth role for me and could lead to more: getting promoted, leading a team, getting paid!

The problem? I Googled them and not a single female in a C-suite leadership role. On LinkedIn, I found very few females in upper management. I told the recruiter I would pass. I had read this story before. I had lived this story before. Knowing how it would end was an easy non-pursuit for me. But the recruiter persisted, and it turned out to be a great move for me. Pause here: this is also a plug to connect with recruiters. The ones that are good at their jobs are your allies and your success is theirs. Not always, but most get paid when you land the job (they help get you there) and most likely you have to stay for a period of time; otherwise, the recruiter has to return a portion of their placement fee from when you took the job. Connecting with recruiters is of no cost to you. In reality they want to meet good candidates because even if they don't have a role you fit today, tomorrow is a new day, a new assignment. Building these relationships is invaluable throughout the lifetime of your career.

Now, back to the story. The recruiter told me not to worry about the current leadership. He shared, after we signed an NDA, that leadership was changing, and I looked up who I would be working with even if the website wasn't updated. He also emphasized that there was enough growth and opportunity within the company that I could be the change I wanted to see. I would be a leader and I would get to hire my team. I could hire for diversity—not just gender but all types. I had an opportunity in front of me to excel, thrive, and earn a leadership role. He helped me see how this was a big upward movement for my career. He was right.

One more quick piece of advice. Remember in Chapter Three a lesson I had to learn the hard way was that a company was not family? That's true. My family has never kicked me to the curb while I was doing my best work, giving them all my energy, and being everything positive I could. A company certainly did. Others in my network have said the same. *They'd tell you to be honest with yourself about what you want in your work culture long term.* There's a difference between a *work family* and *working as a team*. Work does not have to be your whole identity if you don't want that. Any company that tells you they operate like family? Tread lightly. It could be a red flag.

Suffice it to say, culture is important. You should evaluate the current state while also considering what it could be. So how do you begin to evaluate culture?

- When you do research, read reviews.
- Connect with employees on LinkedIn and ask them how they like it. Some won't answer you, others will give a politically correct answer, but you might also get some really good insights that help you in your decision making.
- Is the CEO new? Any of the C-suite executives or upper management?
- Did the marketing and sales leaders who recently joined come from a successful company?
- Are the investors new? Is the board new?
- Is there a new product or solution to take to market?

notes

- Are you seeing multi-year tenure for employees you find on LinkedIn?
- Are customers and potential customers engaging with content online and leaving happy LinkedIn comments? Going to conferences with or hosted by this company?
- Are there public examples of corporate values or simply words on a webpage? Are there pictures on LinkedIn of employees engaged in the company values? Are they volunteering or just saying they are?

These things can signal positive culture. Remember, no one takes on a task thinking, I really want to mess this up. We take on challenges because we want to grow and succeed. If you can find positive moves and happy clients, those are signs of a good culture in place or that one is being developed.

Now, let's begin your research. Choose some industries of interest. If you're not liking what you see, don't bother taking notes about it. Simply note in the margin that it's not for you and why and then complete the activity with industries you are interested in.

What are industries? Telecommunications, automotive, pharmaceuticals, finance and mortgage, banking and credit unions, transportation, high tech/SaaS, consumer services, and government, to name a few. There are sub industries within each category.

Industry	About the Industry	Why I Like It (How It Aligns with Values, Strengths, Energy, and Opportunity)

Now that you have a few industries in mind, let's look at companies within them.

One important thing to consider about companies is the size. Larger companies may have more resources, can be steadier in growth, and be more consistent. They can also be full of red tape or not be as innovative as you'd like. Smaller companies may have fewer resources but the opportunity to grow in both compensation and promotion may be faster. With the good comes the bad, though: they may be more susceptible to economic downs and RIFs. In the Glossary, you'll see terms like *publicly traded company, PE firms, VC firms.* These all refer to ownership. Check out what these terms mean and consider public versus private companies in your research. Just like with company size, there is good and bad with each, and you'll need to decide for yourself. Personally, I have worked for all three types: public companies, private equity companies, and startups backed by venture capital firms.

Depending on who you ask or the article you're reading, the companies that would be labeled as such can change. However, simply being familiar with the concept is enough for you to learn and complete quality research. What are these segments? Startups, enterprise, mid-market, and commercial.

Some people like a 20-person startup where they do eight different jobs on any given day. To put this kindly, folks say you'll "wear many hats." It's a grind, but you stay hoppin'! The largest businesses are commonly referred to as "enterprise." These are the Wal-Marts of the world, Ford Motor Company, and AT&T.

Mid-market or commercial companies are smaller companies. For mid-market, think "medium" and for commercial think, "smallest." Mid-market usually means companies that are about $25 million in revenue to $1 billion valuation. Commercial means any money made at all to approximately $25 million.

Companies also have many ways to segment the market and their client base. For example, number of employees, revenue, or global footprint. I bet you'll see other labels, but they are just that—a way to refer to a specific type of account so everyone working at that company is aligned. If the labels look unfamiliar, look them up and you'll find the answers aren't all that complex.

To make this easier to understand as you get started, pick companies (brands) that you personally like.

- Why do you like them?
- Why do you use this solution or service?
- Why do other people use this solution or service?
- Can you find success stories? Happy clients?

Develop a Growth Mindset and Find What Fits You

notes

- Do they sell to other companies or only to consumers?
- What "good" or "fix" does this bring to the market? To consumers?
- Have you ever visited their website?
- Have you visited their LinkedIn page?
- How are they selling to you?
- What is their brand and message?
- What industry are they in?
- Who else in the market does what they do?
- What else can you find out about the culture of the company?
- Is this a public or private company?
- What can you find out about the success and health of this company?
- Are there philanthropic endeavors?
- Can you feel that DEI is ingrained in the culture or is it a page on the website?

Once you research a few favorite brands, do the same but specifically with education companies: EdTech, educational strategy, and consulting firms who specialize in selling to all levels of learning institutions (primary, secondary, higher ed). These will be the easiest for you to use to draw comparisons. You may not comprehend all the business jargon (refer to the Glossary at the end of the book), but you'll have a deeper understanding of context because you've applied their teaching strategy, used their lesson plan format, used their online gradebook, used their tools for online learning, etc. Then find a few companies that are in the industries you found that you would consider working in.

Then, choose some unfamiliar companies within the industries you are interested in. Don't feel limited to the rows I've provided. If you want to do more research, that's great! The more time you spend here investigating where you will be a good fit, the better chance you have of starting a new career in the right place.

The more you get familiar with the market landscape, understand who the end customer is, and learn how a company generates revenue by solving a problem, selling a product, or delivering a service, the easier this journey will be.

Keep in mind you don't need to go exceptionally deep on your research just yet. Look up a lot of options, get to know what's out there. Once you're more familiar, then you can refine and go back for a second, deeper look.

notes

Company	About the Company	Why I Like It (How It Aligns with Values, Strengths, Energy, and Opportunity)
A favorite brand, product, or solution		
A second favorite brand, product, or solution		
Education or EdTech company		
A second education or EdTech company		
A company in the _____ industry		
A second company in the _____ industry		

Develop a Growth Mindset and Find What Fits You

Data and Metrics

The final piece in developing a business mindset and finding companies, industries, and solutions you align with is to understand what success looks like for these companies. This means looking at metrics and using data to identify success.

Some data is quantitative (numbers), some data is qualitative (categorical).

Personally, I don't think anyone is going to expect you to be a data guru. Even folks with 10+ years of experience constantly learn a new analysis method, data strategy, or approach to what to measure and how. Topics like data, business intelligence tools that display reports and visuals, machine learning, and AI (artificial intelligence) are changing so quickly, everyone is on their toes. Don't overthink this topic. Instead, allow yourself to become familiar with data and learn the basics. Be mindful that data is only useful once collected and analyzed, then turned into information and actionable insights. Data should be used to measure, apply change where needed, and reinforce what's working.

You do this with your student performance scores all the time for reading, math, English...it's the same practice as business. You first assess student performance with a pretest. You then use it to tailor your lesson plans and give extra time to areas where students scored low. You then have formative assessments where you gauge growth and whether the kiddos are on track. You talk to them and ask how they are doing. You continue to tweak lessons based on quantitative and qualitative data. Then you give a summative assessment of a final test and project. You look at the growth between pretests and posttests. Too many failures as a group? You address it and then reassess. Only a few stragglers? They get help before or after school.

Data collection comes from many places, but in your evaluation stage, here are some places to get started:

- Follow business intelligence and AI tool companies on LinkedIn.
- Follow CEO, CRO, or product leaders of the companies or industries you are interested in.
- Watch webinars on data and metrics to see how companies who sell these products are teaching the market to use it to solve problems.
- Watch YouTube videos of these topics. *Truthfully, this is how I taught myself about APIs (application programming interface) and moving data from one system to another for my first job after teaching. As a concept, it is much simpler than you think.*

- Follow earnings reports and watch stock performance.
- Watch webinars in which customers of data products are sharing how they use data.

Keep in mind that you don't have to pursue a job in data, just be familiar enough to talk about how you can use it to improve performance, productivity, and process.

Now What?

My chosen (or desired) committee/activity from "Don't Say No":

What I will be—*or aspire to be*—doing on this committee/activity:

Now, apply the above to any three of the companies from your research (I'd pick what I was MOST interested in if I were you). If it's not clear how they align, you'll have to spend more time researching the company to understand more about what they do, why they do it, how they do it, and who they do it for.

Committee to Company	Measurement (Quantitative and Qualitative)
How my activity participation translates to a business need or outcome.	Here is the data I gathered from my activity participation and what it could mean for business.

Committee to Company	Measurement (Quantitative and Qualitative)
How my activity participation translates to a business need or outcome.	Here is the data I gathered from my activity participation and what it could mean for business.

Committee to Company	Measurement (Quantitative and Qualitative)
How my activity participation translates to a business need or outcome.	Here is the data I gathered from my activity participation and what it could mean for business.

6

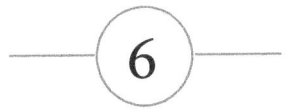

What's Possible?
Discover Your Next Career

If the first question I am asked is "how did I get out of teaching," the second question, too, is almost always the same:

What can I do?

I don't even know what jobs exist.

The answer is, just about anything you set your mind to. Yes, this could require proper qualifications, certifications, education, credentials, but all of those are attainable and don't have to be complicated. Some folks I've spoken with settled on a new career while in the classroom, studied for the required exam for the new role during the school year, and passed the certification exam while teaching so they could start job hunting while still teaching yet qualified to make a change.

That said, most jobs don't require an additional certification. You can obtain professional development for your new non-classroom career no differently than the time you gave to professional development to better your teaching while in the classroom. It simply matters how much passion you have and the amount of effort you are willing to give to learn a new role based on the job you want.

notes

As you read this chapter, think about, and have close, your exercises from Chapters Two and Three. You listed your values, strengths, growth opportunities, and areas where you can get stronger. You identified what drains you at work—essentially what activities or tasks to avoid, or at least minimize, in your next job. You know what energizes you, the tasks that don't even feel like work. Also have close the industry and company research you did. As we narrow down potential jobs, see if the role you want is available at a company you like and what specifics that role has within an industry. No different than a third-grade reading lesson—the end goal is to have children comprehend and read better. But it may look different in execution pending campus or district.

This is how you start to deduce what next job you can have, what you pursue as a next career.

Begin searching for roles that mirror your natural strengths, align with your values and give you energy rather than take from it. Chances are you are unhappy as a teacher because your natural strengths are buried by tasks on your Drain list. The goal of getting a new role should not be to take the first job you get. Real change will require you investing in starting a new career that balances you, fulfills you, and allows you to do what you love.

Now, chances are you won't love everything about your new role. But that's why it's work and not a hobby. And it's also why you don't do it for free.

Instead of asking, "what can I do?" the better question is, "what are the jobs that align to my values and strengths?" Well, I'm no expert, but I took some time to write out jobs and roles I'm familiar with in overarching categories. Some might look at the list below and see departments within a company. And loosely? Sure, that's what they are.

I stuck to entry-level, early-level roles as your years of teaching experience won't necessarily get you a lateral role in management for years working. Don't think of this as a knock on you. This is a bold move you're making. And I'll bet that these entry/early-level roles will pay better, provide more balance, and be enjoyable.

Also keep in mind, my career in regard to management and leadership grew very quickly. In Chapter Ten, others share a very similar experience. I might have entered corporate at the entry level, but I got to a vice president role with 15+ direct reports and cross-functional responsibility much faster than expected due to my entire background, teaching included. You can't necessarily equate the time spent by friends and acquaintances in entry roles to how much time you'll spend. I'll put money on your accelerated growth.

A final note: I chose these categories because this has been my experience. On some I was able to go deep. Others not so much, but I'm familiar with them and have engaged with these groups since leaving teaching. There are more jobs out there; this is a high-level list. If you find what you're interested in, do more research there, beyond what I can offer in this chapter.

> The last bit of advice here: tag team this chapter with Chapter 10 if you haven't skipped ahead at all. When you find the role for you, read the success story.

Customer/Client Success Roles

These are jobs that support a client or customer that uses, consumes, or interacts with the product or service for sale. You are the face of the company for clients. If you work for a B2B company, you'll talk to employees of that company in this role. Most likely it will be the person or few people who manage the tool, product, or service at the company. If you work for a B2C company, you'll talk to folks just like yourself.

Some client roles can be generalist, but very similar customer-facing roles may have a particular focus; for example, implementation will focus on getting a client set up with the solution whereas client manager will handle the ongoing relationship.

Why you'd love it:

You help make the project, product, program, or solution a success! You are the main point of contact for the client; you build the relationship. You can become an extension of the client's team or initiative. You help them succeed.

You can provide valuable support and keep the business relationship fruitful for both the client and the company. If you want a role with menial interaction and where you'd support a lot of accounts and not have so much direct contact with clients, a renewals manager would be a good fit (secure a new contract before the current one expires).

Challenges:

People can be mean. Budgets at companies can be tight. If the project or product or service is not what-who-when-where-why-how it's "supposed" to be or the

notes

client thought it would be, you'll get the brunt of the frustration and anger. You'll need to be good at de-escalating a situation, bringing people back to even, and aligning on a path forward.

You are the main communication stream for most companies to their customers. If things are bad, you have to be positive. You represent the brand, the company. If you can't take a bit of friction at times, you're in the wrong place. But if you have a heart of service and care about making your clients happy, the friction will be minimal.

A typical day:

- Talk to your assigned customers via video conference, phone, and email.
- Answer questions about the product, solution.
- Help submit, monitor, and communicate resolutions of help tickets.
- Do quarterly business reviews—present success and growth opportunities.
- Support securing a renewal for a continued business relationship.
- Support growing the business relationship by suggesting more features and products.
- Join kickoff calls and support implementation communications (not always the owner of the project but you are the central cog in the wheel).
- Communicate news—hopefully good announcements (new product, new webinar), but also share the bad even when difficult (billing issues, data breaches).
- Represent your company and meet up with your clients at conferences or presentations (this is the really fun part!).
- Surprising and delighting customers (as everyone at the company should do!).

Applicable teaching skills:

1. Did you read the de-escalation part? Any misbehaving student or disgruntled parent you've brought back down, centered their emotions? If this was easy for you, you're good at it, it made you feel good to be able to bring a troubling situation into a productive conversation? You'd excel here.
2. The company helps with communications and materials you will share with your assigned customers. You're more of a delivery service and communication catalyst, not unlike using someone else's lesson plan and accompanying materials.
3. Supporting securing the renewal and/or selling more services can be a lot like helping students determine the right course or level for your students for next year. You may only have these students for a year, but you do think

notes

about how they should be supported and successful once they leave your class. Using critical thinking skills and data to support your opinion is very similar in how you'll plan the best course of action for your clients.

Job titles to search for:

- Client or Customer Success Manager (CSM)
- Client or Customer Experience Manager (CXM)
- Implementation Manager
- Onboarding Specialist
- Renewals Manager

Instructional Designer, Content Creator, Marketing Roles

These are jobs that use programs to create content for training, learning, coaching, and communication. These roles are flexible in that most departments in a company need this. However, due to budgets, a few departments will do this for the entire organization. Most likely the training and/or marketing departments will create content for their customers, for prospects, and for internal uses. Gathering the requirements and going through the planning process to make content means talking to various stakeholders and departments within the organization.

To break that down, here are some clear examples:

- Take the technical documentation from the product team about how a new feature works and turn it into a layman's term resource for clients to learn about how to use the new feature. This might be a Word document, a PowerPoint slide, or a video (in which they write the script and support the recording and editing process). You'll take snips, pictures, and screen grabs to accompany the text.
- Create a deck for sales and CSM roles to use with their clients and prospects that explains why your company's solution is better than others, how other clients are finding success, and what industry trend information could be useful.
- Document and add images to a "How-To Guide" or "FAQ" for HR to give all employees to support benefits selection during open enrollment.
- Create one-page "cheat sheets" of client personas (the VP, the director, the system admin) to be used in a training session by the Enablement Team so

notes

your peers who interact with clients know what each person attending the meeting cares about and how to communicate value to them most effectively.

- Develop interactive SCORM files for engaging, clickable training sessions.

Not to mention, the marketing department plans events and plans for employees to attend events. This can be fun work—big conferences, booth prep, and travel. And big conferences are not located in small, boring cities (let's jet to sunny San Diego!).

Why you'd love it:

If you liked using Adobe, Canva, and other software to make engaging materials for your students, or if you find energy in knowing that what you create will help customers and employees, this is for you.

Challenges:

Folks in my network who have these jobs can at times get caught up in the company leadership jumping at what is shiny. There is not always enough time and without a clear line of sight as to why you are being asked to create materials, it can feel like your work doesn't mean as much as it could or should. Maintaining alignment and knowing what KPI or outcome your content is supposed to drive towards can mitigate this substantially.

A typical day:

- Meet with stakeholders and other departments to gather information and requirements for what they need created (a video, a document, a deck, etc.).
- Use software applications to create content.
- Upload content into Wikis, LMS, or any other content repository.
- Meet with other vendors and conference personnel to plan events.

Applicable teaching skills:

1. Are you a tech savvy teacher? Using software is how these materials are created now. You'd use a lot of the same skillset here as you did in the classroom when it comes to Canva, Adobe, and the like.
2. Ensuring you can meet your audience where they are. Not different from meeting your students where they are: training content or marketing materials need to speak to the audience the same way. They need to be tailored to speak to who you need them to. If your information is too high-level, it will not be understood or create interest. Too simple? People scroll past.

notes

3. Tying lessons to state standards is much like aligning requests for content to KPIs. If alignment is missing, you'll find you're constantly pivoting on the purpose of the piece of content and what it's meant to do, and engagement will be low.

Job titles to search for:
- Instructional Designer
- Content Creator/Writer
- Marketing Content Creator
- Events Coordinator
- Content Manager/Administrator
- Content Development Creator

Project Manager

These are jobs that are self-explanatory. Mid- to large-sized companies keep a team (department, if very large) to manage internal and external projects on behalf of the company. The job is to gather what is the project and *why it's needed*, manage everyone and everything throughout the project, provide status updates and risks to leadership and stakeholders, oversee any testing, oversee any communications or rollout plan, and get signoff when the project is launched/complete.

Why you'd love it:

If you enjoy the planning phases of teaching—you like designing lessons and curriculum, you create to-do lists and get a body high and crave that dopamine hit when you cross an item off—then you'll like project management. You see entire projects through from start to finish. You get to see the outcome delivered, the new "thing" implemented, the celebration when it works! I'm sure there are some examples where a project manager has one project, but my guess is you'll have the opportunity (or be required) to manage several projects at the same time. No monotony here but certainly sticking to applying templates and following standard processes.

Challenges:

You can't control others' attitudes, behaviors, or actions, yet as the project manager it is your responsibility to keep everyone on track at the pace necessary to meet the deadline. Almost none of the resources (meaning, people) that are needed to complete the project will report to you. You'll need really strong soft skills and

What's Possilble? Discover Your Next Career

notes

the ability to influence to get everyone marching in the same direction without demanding it. And stay on budget.

Juggling schedules of many folks in different departments can be trying. This can feel like herding cats, and sharing the bad news of delays or over-budget news to anyone is not a fun conversation to have. Again, you don't control the person(s) who didn't deliver on time, but you do deliver the news to leaders and are responsible for keeping milestones on time and almost always have to explain other's choices if there is a delay. But throwing that resource under the bus or oversharing their business? Big no-no. So, acting diplomatically and juggling politics is required. I categorize these tricky conversations as Necessary Evils. You'll need thick skin and confidence (real or imagined!) for these days.

A typical day:

- Host or attend various meetings for requirements: gathering meetings, status meetings, workshop meetings.
- Communicate, both in written form and orally, and update the project plan/tracker.
- Keep track of and document action items, next steps, the budget, and who is going to do what by when.
- Fill gaps. You need to be agile, take on work and do it yourself, and advocate for what's needed to keep folks on time and on task.

Applicable teaching skills:

1. If you used (and hopefully liked) planning tech like Planbook or managing student engagement in Edmodo or Google Classroom, there are some really cool project planning software programs out there. You can really put your organization skills to use in tools like Basecamp, Asana, or monday.com.
2. Coordinated resources for a committee or task force? You were doing the same project management on campus as you'll do in the business world.
3. Applying strong relationship-building skills and the ability to communicate to influence the decisions of others and hold the team accountable.

Job titles to search for:

- Project Manager
- Project Coordinator
- Change Management Coordinator
- Project Administrator

notes

Corporate Trainer, Revenue Enablement

These are jobs that I clearly love the most and were the best fit for me. Entry level enablement roles and corporate training roles are one of the most obvious for teachers exiting the classroom (right up there with content development and instructional design). Why have these roles been the best fit for me? They also integrate learning and coaching software. That isn't always the case—there are plenty of traditional, face-to-face sessions that take place. Take your teaching job and substitute *students* and *classroom* for the business principles I shared earlier.

Teaching:

Aligning lessons to standards, creating content or tweaking out-of-the-box lesson plan materials, delivering to students, assessing and measuring progress, and communicating data (attendance, test scores, project marks) to parents.

⬇

Training:

Aligning training to KPIs, creating content or tweaking marketing materials, delivering to employees, assessing and measuring progress, and communicating data (engagement, knowledge check scores, and practice marks) to managers.

Why you'd love it:

You're still helping. You're still the go-to for people to get better. Many times, folks will share with trainers where they need help. A student who seeks you out to help them understand what they need to go to community college? The really silly student questions, like "what lunch shift am I?" three months into the school year? Employees tend to do the same for the training department and "favorite" trainers. You become a trusted source of knowledge and you're a safe space to

notes

ask the silly questions. No one wants to display their weaknesses, especially not to managers, peers, or customers. The trainer, the enablement manager, the onboarding specialist are the go-to. Besides, you have all the good updates and what the latest is—your training is tied to helping the company employees be able to work in a manner that achieves the company target. And get there fast!

Challenges:

There are usually more requests than time to meet them all. As a teacher, you can relate. But in the corporate world it can be rather difficult to convince a sales manager that she doesn't need six new slides plus training for her team. What she needs is better account planning, and you can help (although I bet she's pretty insistent she will still need those slides. UGH).

Head on a swivel here in this role, especially if it's more enablement than a training-only role. With training, you'll get apathy and lack of participation, and it can be hard to get tenured, veteran employees to engage in a meaningful way. Dealing with a student who is checked out during your class? So much easier than dealing with his dad who is acting the same at a training session. The apples do not fall far...

Also, don't get sucked into compliance training. It's a total snooze and everyone is annoyed by it. Let HR and legal keep that.

A typical day:

- Set up session invites and share the agenda in advance.
- Plan and create materials for before, during, and after sessions.
- Deliver training sessions and put the content in the LMS. You might even assign the courses or help/own admin of the LMS.
- Bonus points for companies that have enablement-specific platforms (similar to LMS).
- Meet with leaders to gain clarity on strategy and why they believe training or programming on a particular topic should happen.
- Measure practice attempts by attendees, answer questions, and reinforce information.
- Run reports and pull data.
- Coach others during reinforcement sessions (required) or office hours (optional sessions).
- Analyze performance data and develop a point of view on what's needed based on metrics and share this with leaders (when this happens, it feels pretty cool).

notes

Applicable teaching skills:

1. Breaking down topics to various levels to meet training attendees where they are and build upon that (Maslow's, DOK charts, etc.), and making and delivering training materials to attendees.
2. Measuring level of understanding and identifying skill level (businesses use competency matrices for roles much like you'd use a rubric to help a student understand how you measured their performance or project).
3. Much like communicating a student grade to parents both informally (email them) and formally at a parent-teacher conference, you'll communicate an employee's performance to their manager both informally (email them) and in booked meetings. There are a lot of similarities in needing parent and manager support to get a student or employee where they should be—need to be—if they are to be successful and move forward.

Job titles to search for:

- Corporate/HR Trainer
- Sales Trainer
- Product Trainer
- Enablement Specialist
- Enablement Manager
- Enablement Program Manager
  (same as above but specific to a topic, e.g., onboarding)

Because this has become my career, and my enablement network might disown me if I don't clarify: revenue enablement is not sales training. Training is one piece of the larger role of enablement. Chances are, though, that as an entry-level enablement team member or manager, you will be doing more of the execution practice of training and coaching to a methodology more than analysis and planning. A true sales trainer role would also be a great first step before getting into enablement roles.

Department Specialists

These are jobs that, depending on what you're certified in, rely more on an application of the subject content more so than your teaching skills. This is probably more applicable to middle school and high school teachers looking to transition.

notes

When I think of this topic, I think of my friend Christian (you'll meet him in Chapter Ten). He took his math skills to the corporate world and used them to become an actuary in the insurance industry.

Why you'd love it:

If you really love your subject area but at the end of college didn't know what job that could be and eventually chose (or fell into) teaching as the outlet, this would be you. You can find a corporate role that speaks to your subject strengths and love of the material that is not classroom teaching. You're the person who, when the students ask "why do we even need this?" are able to list a bunch of job titles. So take your own advice and what jobs/reasons you give your students, and start looking into it.

Challenges:

It's hard to know what you want to be when you grow up. And changing jobs can feel (and even be) risky. To take the more "subject matter expert" route and not rely on your teaching skills as much to get your next job will be more of a challenge. You'll really have to think about what stories you can tell to get a job based on your subject knowledge. That said, teaching has given you plenty of applicable corporate roles experience.

A typical day:

- Job dependent, BUT I'm sure you can bank on:
- Attending and hosting meetings.
- Keeping your team and manager informed of your progress and what you're working on.
- Being a great teammate and sharing the workload and taking on more responsibilities if the situation calls for it (next time, it's their turn).

Applicable teaching skills:

1. Figuring out how and why your daily work supports the outcome.
2. Soft skills: organization, time management, communication, relationship building.
3. Using your critical thinking and problem-solving skills.

Job titles to search for:

- Actuary or Analyst (math teachers)
- Lab, Testing Roles (science teachers)

notes

- Paralegal, Legal Support Roles (English teachers)
- RFP, Proposal Manager (English teachers)
- Coordinator Roles in Operations, HR, Product, Finance (very organized personalities)
- Office Manager (good at connecting people and resources, social personalities)
- LMS Admin for HR, Enablement, or any Tech Admin (tech savvy teachers)

Sales, Revenue Roles (And Not Just Real Estate)

These are jobs that engage with clients and/or potential clients (prospects) and in which you explain how a product or service meets the company's (B2B) or individual consumer's (B2C) needs or fixes a problem.

The typical progression of a sales career will look something like this:

ENTRY ROLE

Sales/Business/Account Development Representative
You learn the basics and get the customer to agree to a meeting. You hand it over to the Sales Representative.

Account Manager
Grow in the partnership a client has with the company by selling necessary, additional services.

MID LEVEL

Graduate to a Sales Representative or Account Executive
Now you're a Closer. You pick up the conversation where the Development Rep. left off. Getting the contract signed is your responsibility.

Customer Success Manager
Own the day-to day relationship.

Or Make a Pivot to

HIGHER LEVEL

Get promoted to Sales Director
These jobs are usually seling into Enterprise and strategic (meaning high importance due to potential growth or logo) customers.

Solution Specialist Role
Own the design, demonstration, and trial of the solution presented to the customer.

What's Possilble? Discover Your Next Career

notes

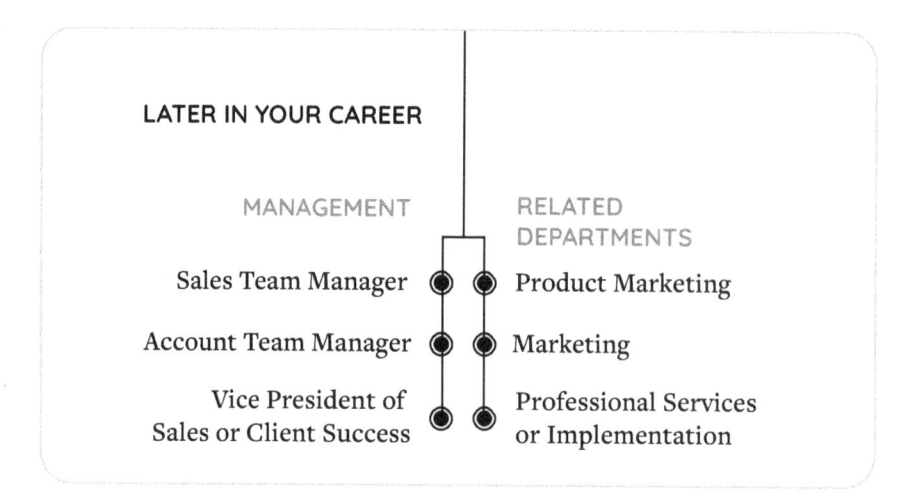

LATER IN YOUR CAREER

MANAGEMENT	RELATED DEPARTMENTS
Sales Team Manager	Product Marketing
Account Team Manager	Marketing
Vice President of Sales or Client Success	Professional Services or Implementation

The sky's the limit for a successful sales professional: become senior vice president, run an account management team, switch over to product marketing or marketing, or run the client support team.

Why you'd love it:

It's challenging; there is real competition. When done right, you do help others fix a problem. You can help make your clients and other companies successful. You carry a quota and can make a lot of money for you, your family, and your future if you exceed it. Monetary and title promotions can come quickly; great sales reps are always in demand (have I mentioned businesses are all about driving revenue?).

There are options. You can "hunt" for new customers, you can "farm" accounts that are already customers and grow them. You can work in different segments: small clients, medium, and large. You can sell into industries you find interesting. Once you get good with one product/solution, you can sell related ones. See how quickly growth opportunities can present themselves?

Challenges:

Sales seems to be a main de facto career conversation for teachers. I understand why, or at least I know why it appealed to me (Getting paid? It's me, hi.) Sales has so much familiarity with our society. But if you're not passionate about the solution you sell? If you don't actually believe in the product you're offering? If you don't know why or how the product/solution fixes problems? People can see right through it and success will be hard to come by. That's not to say you won't close a few deals, but I am saying you won't hit those really lucrative commissions opportunities.

Knowing all the use cases and how your product/solution is a fit takes real work. You'll need to put in the time to research, learn, and get to know your client—all while the company is pushing you to sell bigger, faster, stronger.

The salesperson who is trying to convince you the jalopy is AirPlay-compatible? The additional, additional insurance if a hurricane hits your home when you live in Utah? Yeah, no one likes that slimy, say-what-I-need-to-to-get-your-money salesperson. Moreover, if you don't take the time to learn your market, product features, and why a customer or consumer needs what you're selling, you won't be able to answer questions. This creates doubt and potentially discredits you in the eyes of the customer, especially if you make up answers. Your company really won't like that part where you make it up either. How the heck can they deliver on what doesn't exist? You can tell when your students didn't read the chapter—consumers can tell when you didn't either.

Another challenge: there is real competition. And that quota can feel like a monkey on your back and missing it means PIP (Performance Improvement Plan). You can be let go pretty easily if you miss your sales target a few quarters in a row, certainly if you miss a few years in a row. Good companies will coach and help before letting you go, but sadly, that's usually not the case.

A typical day:

- Interact with clients, prospects.
- Prep for, communicate about, set the agenda for, and host sales meetings.
- Meet with your development representative to plan who they call and what they say.
- Manage your book of business and meet with a solution specialist—who are you solutioning the product for? Why do they care? What benefits can you bring?
- Attend training sessions, practice and dry-run your pitches, attend office hours.
- Attend meetings with your clients. You might meet with the implementation team on a deal you're close to closing, you might attend the kickoff call with a new client and be there when they meet their CSM, or you might attend an internal meeting on support tickets if your client is experiencing an ongoing issue and you need to push for quick resolution.

Applicable teaching skills:

1. Multi-tasking. This doesn't mean being constantly distracted, but rather you have multiple deals and opportunities in play at the same time and communicate with various others within the company.
2. Presentation skills and explaining why something is important, the impact it can have.
3. Process orientation. Much like you have classroom procedures, the sales process is the same. It's the same stages but can be different each time. Here is what I mean: you probably had classroom procedures that used an "exit ticket" and students couldn't stand or line up at the door before the bell rang. However, the question on the exit ticket was different daily. In sales, the stages will be the same. You'll start with discovery—this means you ask about their company and what they need help with. The questions you ask will be different depending on who you are talking to (a manufacturing customer will care more about OSHA regulation and government compliance whereas a bank might care more about data security). This is not to say manufacturing doesn't care about data security and banks don't care about compliance, but it's what you ask about first that matters.

Job titles to search for:

- Business Development Representative (BDR)
- Account Development Representative (ADR)
- Sales Development Representative (SDR)
- Sales Representative
- Account Executive
- Account Manager
- Renewal Manager, Coordinator

All of these roles may also have a market or segment attached to them and will determine who you are selling to or supporting. I mentioned these in Chapter Five—enterprise, mid-market, commercial, and startups. Enterprise sales is usually not the entry level. You'll find startups and smaller companies are more likely to give you a shot. This is great as you will learn so much. You can then take that experience and go after those larger, more lucrative mid-market and enterprise sales roles.

Solution Specialists

(aka Solution Engineer, Solution Consultant, Solution Architect)

These are jobs that explain how or why a product or service is helpful to the client. This role supports sales, sales reps, account managers, or a CSM who is looking to add additional services for their assigned clients. You usually don't have a quota, but you are the go-to teammate that the seller and CSM will count on. You are the product/solution expert.

The client is also aware you don't hold the quota. Clients don't always believe the seller because, well, they need to make the sale! As a solution specialist, you are the Truth Teller, the one they trust, the person who will give the "real" answer.

Why you'd love it:

It's sales, and that makes it competitive. Let's be real, if a company does not make money, it won't exist. Now don't get all existential and mired down in the pitfalls of capitalism and the 1%. If you want a challenge (selling against other companies, solutions) but also want to be seen as the "expert" and the specialist with the answers, this is for you.

You'll also get to interact with the product team, IT teams, and implementation to ensure the demonstration you are about to give is viable and correct. If you loved learning the back end of the LMS and your other classroom tech to figure out how it worked, this will be a lot of fun.

Challenges:

It can be high pressure. Sales teams are meant to close deals. Sure, you won't win them all, but you certainly can't have a pattern of losses. And pending your background, these roles can get technical fast. And if a deal is mis-sold, you're on the list to ask about it. The implementation and delivery teams will not take kindly to a lot of errors or poor explanations of how the product actually works and not sharing the limitations up front.

Be prepared to study hard and put in the time to learn depending on the complexity of the product you're supporting for sales.

A typical day:

- Research your market and what's new in the industry. Join webinars.
- Join external meetings with partners, other vendors, and clients.

notes

- Join internal meetings—prep with your peers, practice/dry-run the meeting (especially for high-profile clients or prospects).
- Practice and deliver solution/product demonstrations.
- Answer questions via phone and email and put your notes in the required company system.
- Participate in ongoing training hosted by the company and sales teams.
- Support a client or prospect during a test or trial of the solution/product.
- Support RFP/RFI (request for proposal, request for information) efforts (filling out a questionnaire).

Applicable teaching skills:

1. Checking for understanding and presentation skills. When on any call with a client, be it pre- or post-sales, ensuring everyone is following along and has the same understanding is critical for any project's success. This goes for internal meetings as well. As the specialist, you'll present materials, products, and documentation that others in the meetings will need.
2. Putting in the time to become an expert. Teachers are used to putting in the extra work to get deeper understanding to answer student questions and share additional material to increase engagement. We are natural life-long learners. Putting in the extra time to act as the trusted solution expert will be required for these roles.
3. Oral and written communication. In any role these are needed, but in a role in which you are clarifying to the others in the meeting or via email, your communication has to be better than your average person. Communicating in a clear, succinct, and simple way is what teachers are good at while also ensuring folks comprehend the material.

Job titles to search for:

- Solution Consultant (more discussion of how it will work, less technical products and solutions)
- Solution Architect (more building involved, setting up sample product sites)
- Solution Engineer (more technical, even more building which could mean connecting systems and understanding concepts like APIs)
- Solution Specialist (can be a combination of all three of the above)

Regarding which label does what, this is my opinion based on my experience. As you research, others may define the solution roles differently. The point here is that some are technical, some are more about building, and some are about storytelling and experiences.

Now What?

FIRST:

- Note what jobs interested you the most.
- Search for those titles on LinkedIn Jobs.
- Search for those titles on the websites of companies of interest.

Now, pull all your prior activities together:

- What job(s) aligned to your values, strengths, energy, and opportunities?
- How can you practice the necessary job skills while participating in your "Don't Say No"?
- List your top five transferable skills from the classroom to the job you want. Use what you documented in the Chapter Four Bonus Exercise.

Consider the following as you jot down notes in the second column:

- Is the skill exactly the same or does it change slightly?
- Is the audience/recipient of the skill the same or different?
- Are the classroom teacher skills used in corporate but go by another name?
- How are the successes and outcomes measured differently?
- What information is in the job description to help you compare and contrast?

Classroom Skill	What It Looks Like at the Job I Want

Classroom Skill	What It Looks Like at the Job I Want

Later, we will discuss the best approach to apply for open positions. For now, just search, but if you find a good one, bookmark the page and/or keep the URL close.

SECOND:

Imagine you can interview someone currently in the role you want or someone who had the entry role you want and has built a career from this first job. Write a list of questions you would ask them.

Here are some ideas, but make this your own:

1. What was their career path? Their start?
2. What advice they would give you?
3. What did they like and loathe about the role?
4. What would they do differently if they could?
5.
6.
7.
8.
9.
10.

Ready to be bold? Find people on LinkedIn with the job title you want and connect with them. Start to build the relationship. You'll be limited to 300 characters, so choose your words wisely. What can you say? Tell them you're looking to connect with others in the industry, in the role you want, or you'd like to someday work at the same company. It doesn't have to be a lot. Just a simple hello and why connecting is beneficial. Once you're connected, you can ask if they are open to chatting more about their role, the company, or the industry. Lean on the questions you prepared.

Not ready yet? I'll give you a pass for now because we'll talk about networking and outreach in just a bit, but you are going to have to connect with people. And keep in mind that you have absolutely nothing to lose by asking. They don't reply? So what?

Add a note to your invitation ✕

LinkedIn members are more likely to accept invitations that include a personal note.

> Ex: We know each other from...

0/300

Cancel Send

PUTTING YOUR PLAN TO ACTION

7

Building a Personal Brand
and Telling a Story

This chapter is meaty! You're going to need to spend a bit of time here and this is one of those topics that will evolve with you as your career progresses. It's a good thing, but when I was a teacher, this was NOT on my radar. The teachers I talk to today don't have a personal brand or barely have LinkedIn. Nothing wrong with that, but if you are starting at zero, don't let the volume of new content overwhelm you.

> *Me in 2014: Personal brand? I don't know her.*
> *Me in 2018: A pERsOnaL bRAnD. Eww. Stuck up much?* 😐
> *Me in 2024: Successful careers stem from a strong, clear personal brand.*

notes

I did not love the idea of a personal brand when I first noticed it was a "thing." I think it was around 2014 when I was job hunting that I became aware of personal brands, but I didn't know that's what I was seeing. I saw them in action more when I began using LinkedIn more in 2015 after starting my first post classroom job. It was only after my first corporate job that I realized how powerful LinkedIn was and what it could be used for. I saw personal brands as a show of expertise, knowledge, and work experiences, yet somehow it felt like chest thumping and "look at me" sales of oneself.

Couple my lack of experience with my immaturity about social media for professional reasons versus personal and social? All I knew was that I needed to be "careful" when it came to what I posted on Facebook as there were teachers who faced (and still face) undeserved scrutiny, judgment, and consequences for the decisions they make on the internet. My ignorance was high and I was unable to understand what a "personal brand" actually was, what a good one looked like, how to create and cultivate one, or how it was something that could help me.

Like I said, at first it sounded gross to me—this concept of personal brand. It felt like I was being pompous, showy, and desperate for attention. I only understood personal brands to be a professional Facebook thirst trap and later, Instagram influencers. But at work. For a person like me with something to prove in my career (that I was to be taken seriously and belonged in the corporate world) and not active on professional social outlets, it didn't connect for me. Those feelings morphed into indignation: I am NOT for sale.

Except, as time passed, *I realized I kind of am*. We all are **when it comes to our careers.** (Don't take this down a rabbit hole, please. Keep it high level, about skills and paid work).

> **We just need to remember that we have a choice.**

My time is available for a price. My business talents are available for a price. My teaching techniques, ability to coach and motivate folks to learn, and professional experiences are all available for a price. It's for **"sale"** in that I give it to whom and what I choose because I get compensation in return.

And people **buy** what they like, what they care about, what they see value in, and what and who they connect with. You know this already. In practice this is any time you are a consumer.

Personal brands are not to be confused with an inflated ego, obnoxious behavior, or a gross exaggeration of talents and capabilities. Rather, it is a way to frame what you are willing to offer up, who you are, and your skill set and perspectives. Relay that to your career. Talent scouts and hiring managers will hire who they can trust, who they see value in, and who would be a good company culture fit. Stopping here to say very loudly to you: I AM NOT TALKING ABOUT YOUR *RESUME* ALONE. That is only one lever to pull regarding communication of your personal brand.

Recall how I encouraged you in Chapter Four to get involved in something while teaching that is part of a larger play to segue into business—to tell a leadership story, a success story, a story of how you used your critical thinking to solve a problem and the outcomes you made happen. Take that same approach but apply it to your LinkedIn account: what you post for all to see and what notes/DMs you send using the platform can help you and support your goal of leaving the classroom. That work is part of a larger, longer play to set you up for success.

You will share your personal brand on LinkedIn, in webinar chat rooms, and in professional development communities on Slack. I'll talk more on this later and how to go about participating, heck, even knowing what to join!

You need to be able to help others understand who you are and be able to articulate this in a succinct manner: who you are, what you want, and why you're the right fit. It's storytelling.

Putting that story to work once you craft it—now you're networking.

Let's start with the basics. What do these words and phrases mean?

notes

	Definitions	Take Action
Personal Brand	Technically, "personal brand" is not a word, rather two definitions together to create a concept. It should be crafted based on your personal values. **Personal**[4] **: ADJ,** *relating to, or affecting a particular person; relating.* **Brand**[5] **: N,** *a public image, reputation, or identity conceived of as something to be promoted.*	Determine this: what do you want the market and future employers to know about you before they even meet you? Then ⬇
Storytelling[6]	**Storyteller: N,** *a relater of anecdotes.* **Relate**[7] **: V,** *to give an account of; tell.* **Anecdote**[8] **: N,** *a usually short narrative of an interesting, amusing, or biographical incident.*	Turn your notes and bullet points from above into a story. Then ⬇
Networking[9]	**Networking: N,** *the cultivation of productive relationships for employment or business.*	Tell your story at conferences, happy hours/lunches, and in email and LinkedIn messages. Then ⬇

---

4   Merriam-Webster. (n.d.). Personal. In Merriam-Webster.com dictionary. Retrieved November 18, 2023,, from https://www.merriam-webster.com/dictionary/personal

5   Merriam-Webster. (n.d.). Brand. In Merriam-Webster.com dictionary. Retrieved November 18, 2023,, from https://www.merriam-webster.com/dictionary/brand

6   Merriam-Webster. (n.d.). Storyteller. In Merriam-Webster.com dictionary. Retrieved November 18, 2023,, from https://www.merriam-webster.com/dictionary/storyteller

7   Merriam-Webster. (n.d.). Relate. In Merriam-Webster.com dictionary. Retrieved November 18, 2023,, from https://www.merriam-webster.com/dictionary/relate

8   Merriam-Webster. (n.d.). Anecdote. In Merriam-Webster.com dictionary. Retrieved November 18, 2023,, from https://www.merriam-webster.com/dictionary/anecdote

9   Merriam-Webster. (n.d.). Networking. In Merriam-Webster.com dictionary. Retrieved November 18, 2023,, from https://www.merriam-webster.com/dictionary/networking

notes

	Definitions	Take Action
Live an Authentic Professional Life	Well-adjusted humans grow and change with experiences and new information. Determining who you are right now, your brand, doesn't mean it's forever. People are complex and change is okay but remember, your brand is rooted in your personal values (which tend to be stable). **Authentic**[10] **: ADJ,** *not false; true to one's own personality, spirit, or character.* **Professional**[11] **: ADJ,** *having a particular profession as a permanent career.* **Profession**[12] **: N,** *a calling requiring specialized knowledge, intensive preparation.*	Be your brand at your current job too. Don't let your disinterest in teaching or desire to leave distract you from growing and reaching your ultimate goal.

* Definitions created from Merriam-Webster's Dictionary

The rest of this chapter is pretty simple to follow, but if you don't have a LinkedIn account at all and have never even thought about this before, it will be quite a bit of work, I won't lie to you. The good news is, if you follow the recommendations in this chapter, you'll know exactly what to display as public to help you. I'm going to walk you through some of the presentation and coaching I give on developing your story based on the brand you have or want, as well as building a network that is not full of strangers.

This topic is fun for me because I am still a work in progress. Every time I give a presentation on this topic, I leave feeling energized. Not unlike my classroom teaching days, I almost always have self-feedback on how to make it better, or different, or more relatable. Old habits die hard. But I am finally hearing my own advice too and I refine my strengths, my areas of growth and opportunity, and my success stories in a way that excites others.

---

10   Merriam-Webster. (n.d.). Authentic. In Merriam-Webster.com dictionary. Retrieved November 18, 2023,, from https://www.merriam-webster.com/dictionary/authentic

11   Merriam-Webster. (n.d.). Professional. In Merriam-Webster.com dictionary. Retrieved November 18, 2023,, from https://www.merriam-webster.com/dictionary/professional

12   Merriam-Webster. (n.d.). Profession. In Merriam-Webster.com dictionary. Retrieved November 18, 2023, from https://www.merriam-webster.com/dictionary/profession

Building a Personal Brand and Telling a Story

notes

Designing Your Personal Brand

Your personal brand is sharing who you want to be in your next career and beyond. Storytelling is how you deliver this message. We address that in just a bit. Your personal brand is for you to decide.

Some folks will choose to make their personal brand strictly professional. Others will include A LOT of their personal life. I'll share my opinion here, something to ponder and keep in mind. Sharing personal aspects of yourself in the corporate world, making it part of your personal brand, should not be taken lightly. I really want you to consider the long-term impact the oversharing of personal information can have. Not to mention, you're creating a very limited boundary of what would be "off limits" for others to comment on, especially unwelcome comments. As you design yours, it may feel natural to add details about your private life, but consider these questions:

- You
    - Is that you or is that the environment you are in?
    - What happens if you move, whether it's your decision or not?
    - What happens if your significant other loses their job and your standard of living changes?
    - What happens if you encounter (personally or those in your life) legal troubles?

- Your relationships
    - What happens if you get separated/divorced?
    - What happens if your partner leaves you? What if your choices are the cause/reason?
    - What happens if your relationship with your children changes in a negative way?
    - What happens if your relationship with your parents or in-laws changes?

- Your health
    - What happens if your health—physical, mental, emotional—changes?
    - What happens if you or a loved one develops a really bad habit?
    - What happens if you or a loved one develop a struggle with substance abuse?

- Will sharing this information cause immediate bias against you?
    - Will sharing generate pity or judgment and will that anger you?

- Will sharing take away an opportunity before it's even offered?

Even though negative reactions may be wrong or unfair, we cannot pretend it does not happen.

Life is messy. Things happen. But if you don't want to risk having to explain yourself or you haven't thought about one, two, five years down the road, the long term, you should. Most people will find comfort in the middle; sharing professional goals and talents mixed with a bit of high-level private life. My point is, don't overexpose yourself. That detail that takes away the opportunity before it's even offered? You might be okay with that because that's not the culture you seek. But in most cases, your private life is just that, private. My advice? Keep what you share at a very high level. Put effort into finding other ways to relate to people and shared experiences that don't require you to put everything on display.

But I want to draw a clear line here. A personal brand is NOT, nor should it be, what you post on Facebook, Instagram, and other social media. Influencers and our collective social distancing hangover from COVID have made people think they need to, and should, tell all. This influx of personal information on LinkedIn is getting to be a lot. My opinion is that you really should not.

What makes this really difficult is that oversharing is a spectrum. What makes one person uncomfortable may not make another think twice. However, no matter where you fall on the spectrum, there is always risk that is out of your control. What you are okay with, a hiring manager or a company may not be. Your intent may not be the message received by others.

Unsure if this is you? At the risk of making a few folks mad, here are some very real stories and examples that have had an impact. I'm sure you can suspect I've included some direct and indirect personal experiences as well as close friends' experiences below. Proceed with caution.

> **If all of your social media is public and your LinkedIn and Facebook (and other social media) accounts are begging to blend...**

...and you share pictures of your sick child with a snotty nose and fevered, red face? More food for thought, shouldn't your child have consent? Would you want that image of you out there? Post images from hospital beds and info about private medical information? This would be an overshare.

...and you post when you and another adult are in a spat of any kind (your spouse, extended family member, parent, frenemy)? Overshare.

notes

...and you put pictures of your car and home on social media but never pause to ensure you're not showing license plates or addresses of yours, your family, or your neighbors? An unedited picture of your child's driver's license? Post without taking time to ensure other people's privacy is not violated? Oversharing.

...and you've announced you're at the airport and headed to Cancun for the upcoming week because you deserve it and "peace out to bad weather"? I hope your home security system works.

...and post pictures of you/your social group *overindulging* in alcohol even if it is a birthday, anniversary, graduation, or a team win? Overshare.

What professors warned you in college about your social media choices? That's still true in business. And when your X (formerly known as Twitter), Facebook, Instagram, and LinkedIn are all in the same name, searchable on Google, and profile/posts are public? Your personal brand is mostly professional, but it is you. And if people decide to look you up—recruiters, hiring managers, potential teammates, HR—what you thought was private or didn't consider an overshare is now part of that brand. Like it or not, people judge, *especially when they don't even know you.*

I understand that our private lives shape us at work. I really do. You should not have to hide that you are gay, or sober, or overcame a hard time in your life. Or that you are currently having a hard time. The parent of a special needs child lives and experiences parenthood on a completely different level than the rest of parents. The best parents find themselves in the throes of societal punishment and backlash for their kid's TikTok video—27 seconds and BAM!! you're in the fire. A broken marriage for *almost* any reason sucks for EVERYONE. Be adults about this—it is hard on all sides if you view it from the center rather than only your corner. The hardships of people of color, minorities in any way, and LGBTQ+ have experiences much different than the majority. If you don't like this part, that's fine, I'm almost done discussing it, **but I cannot stress enough that if you're not ready to talk about the challenging times publicly when your audience is strangers and employment is at stake, keep private items private.**

Still don't believe me? Tell me, how many lifestyle influencers have gone down in flames due to a breakup, substance abuse, or rejection from children? How many celebrities, athletes, or CEOs have experienced a downfall for personal information? How many careers have we heard about being derailed by online posts and activity? How many women do you know who openly shared they were pregnant in an interview AND got a job offer? How many teachers have lost their jobs over online activity and opinions shared in comments?

No, it's not right, but I keep telling you, business is not your friend nor your family. Companies avoid small risks, and they certainly back away from large ones.

Share that you overcame a challenge, have a belief in spirituality/faith/religion, are a parent, a partner, a spouse. Probably want to stop somewhere near here.

On the flip side, don't make up a story or exaggerate an experience so much so that it is no longer true. Once you find your groove in the corporate world, you learn more about the world around you, and **then you can decide to share more**. Think of it as a kindergarten construction paper project: glue and glitter can always be added. Too much glue and glitter out of the gate is NOT going back in that bottle. Just not going to happen.

Solve your challenge to get out of teaching, get the job first. Then put in the time to change the system. *Plenty of allies are waiting for you once you've arrived.*

The most important standards to keep in mind regarding personal brand are to keep it authentic and professional.

Design Checklist

Decide who you want the market to understand you to be professionally. Here are a few items to consider so you can get started. Heads up, this will most likely be, and probably should be, a work in progress for a bit. When you begin sharing, I'm sure you'll get real-world feedback that will help you make positive improvements and refine in a meaningful way.

- What are your core values?
    - How do those values apply to how you see yourself contributing to a company generating revenue and, more importantly, satisfied clients?
    - How do they apply to how you want to interact with customers and coworkers?
    - How will they continue or improve the culture of a company?
    - How will they impact how you deal with challenges and conflict (because conflict is unavoidable in the longevity of your career, teaching included)?
    - How are they related to your strengths and successes, and what gives you energy?
- Where are you successful? Where are you good? What are your strengths?

notes

- Can you help others be good at it too?
- Can you share a path to help?
- What natural traits and habits do you have that contributed?
- What skills did you have to work hard to develop to experience success?
- What project(s) did you contribute to or own that you are proud of? Why?

- What causes do you care about?
  - Where do you volunteer? Why?
  - What impact are you driving towards?
  - Where and why do you donate?
  - What change/good are you driving towards?
  - Where do you see change needed? Are you working to help?
  - What are you working on that is bigger than yourself?
  - This is a natural place to weave in high-level personal work (coaching kids, mentoring other adults, access/equity of opportunity).

- Where have you invested in yourself both formally (a degree, a certification) and informally (reading, professional development)?
  - What were you looking to solve/improve for yourself?
  - What are your areas of opportunity?

- What do you love *about* your work? (I asked *about your work*, not "do you love work." No one loves work, we have to do that. I'm asking about the *about* part).

- What challenge(s) have you overcome?
  - If you do not include your journey out of teaching, you're nuts! Career transitions are hard when switching from one business field to another. Selling from one industry into another is a challenge. Learning the process and tools from one company to the next takes time. Leaving teaching to get into the corporate world? That's real resilience.
  - Here is where you can weave in some high-level personal story of adversity.

- What is a lesson you've learned the hard way?
  - What can you share and offer to others so they avoid the same mistakes?
  - Here is another place where you can weave in a high-level personal story.

Interested in seeing my personal brand? Check out my LinkedIn. What I share in my About section, the banner photo, the content/posts I've pinned, what I post and comment on, and the organizations I volunteer with all make up my brand. At a

notes

networking event, these would be the things I talk about. I am motivated to coach others to peak performance, support teachers as a career change catalyst, strive to get more women in the workplace, and advocate for the revenue enablement profession.

Another way to accelerate getting started is to use all the great research and thought you've put into the exercise from each chapter. Your personal brand should absolutely call out and play into your strengths. You should add your values and how they relate to the industries and companies you serve or would like to. The jobs you are pursuing are because of some natural strength, skills, drive, or tendency. Use those ideas to start. Don't be afraid to use your notes and get a draft one.

Storytelling

When I present and coach on this topic I start with the good news: humans inherently love stories. Especially if we can learn something, relate, contribute, and see ourselves in the story. To address this, we'll begin with a framework for what "good" stories have in them. It is this story you craft that you'll need in Chapter Nine when we discuss networking, outreach, and interviews. You will tell stories that articulate your brand, the career path you want, and the successes you've already achieved. Storytelling is how others will get to know the professional you. All it takes is practice, then the guts to deliver.

Framework to Tell a GREAT Story

Stories Matter.

- Tell the punchline first, the outcome
- Make it relatable, who/what are you helping
- Keep the middle short
- Stay on topic - all relate back to the punchline
- Use facts, metrics to support
- Consider cause and effect
- Laughter is best
- Timing is better - especially if you're not funny
- Draw on the five senses - engage people
- PRACTICE: Record yourself, read the transcript
- Gain confidence

And For Your Resume.

- Outcomes only
- Be brief
- Use metrics and data

Write your sentence, then flip it:

Served as Department Head from 2019 to 2021 where I revamped the 7th grade math curriculum while teaching, overall student improvement.

3% increase in overall 7th grade math scores while serving as Department Head between 2019-2021.

Building a Personal Brand and Telling a Story

notes

Chances are this will be information you already know or are aware of, especially if you teach/taught any grade-level English writing concepts, told stories of events and people during social studies classes, or taught an elective where much discussion took place. If you were an elementary teacher, you must have read thousands of stories depending on the length of your career and you addressed basic English concepts and told stories during social studies time.

I used to LOVE to tell stories about crazy, lame, unpredictable kings and queens, especially Henry VIII. What a nut job he was! I used to LOVE a good Socratic seminar with my students. My students could write and present information at a deeper level after prepping and then asking a ton of questions the class period(s) before. You'll do the same for telling your story in the voice of your personal brand.

Here is what I believe could/should be included in telling a good story:

- Make it relatable.
- Tell the punchline first.
- Keep the middle short.
- Stay on topic.
- Use facts and metrics to support where possible.
- Consider cause and effect.
- Laughter is good…
- Good timing is better.
- Draw on the five senses.

Then:

- PRACTICE. Record yourself; read the transcript.
- KEEP PRACTICING. Become more succinct; stop with the filler words.
- AND DO IT ONE MORE TIME. Gain confidence.

Let's break each of these pieces down, because you don't need ALL of them, but pending your message, using some or most of these suggestions will help you. I grouped them together because they do naturally support each other, but keep in mind that these are suggestions and as you read why each is important and the impact it can have, choose what you do and don't want to use.

Also, you may tell different aspects of your story to various people. For example; someone may be more familiar with your journey out of teaching because their sister or significant other wants to do the same, and others may need a version where you get much more detailed about the challenge of this journey as they are far removed from the value a teacher brings to corporate roles (they only know their kid did not like their third grade teacher, and personally? They cannot stand Mrs. Teacher from when they were in third grade either). Having multiple versions of how you tell the story and what you highlight does not make it disingenuous. It's you being prepared for all audiences and situations. You'd prepare to deliver information this way to your students (meet them where they are: learning styles, preferences, pretest marks), so don't overthink it.

Crafting Your Story

Make it relatable.

Know your audience. To do this, I hope you take the time to ask them some questions first. If you're prepping for a networking event, take a look at who it's advertised to. Chances are that's who will show up, so plan for that target audience. As mentioned before, simply showing interest in others is a great way to break the ice. It makes who you are talking to feel valued (someone wants to know about them too! And they are just as nervous at this event as you are!). It gives you time to breathe and being a good listener means you are focused on them and not your nerves. Nice way to trick your brain! But the real value comes from learning about them. Now you know a small bit about what they care about, or their career desires, the job they currently have—you know *at least something* about them because they spoke first. And if offered up, most people will speak first. Even if they offer for you to speak first, if you ask them a question—huzzah! They spoke first! We are human, after all, and we do love to gab about ourselves. It's in our nature.

Now that you can relate to them in some small way:

- Do you both want new jobs?
- What have they tried and found success in? Avoid?
- Did they just take on a new role? You can learn from their experience!
- Are you interested in the same type of market, companies, solutions, or roles?

Consider starting your story with what commonalities you have.

Tell the punchline first.

Now that you know where to start, tell the good part first—the ending, the success, the celebration. Sharing good news gets people to lean in.

I used to listen to Paul Harvey with my dad as he drove me to elementary school each morning. Probably on 1120 KMOX or The Big 550. I used to love Paul's stories,

notes

and some (probably most!) went over my head. But he had a great voice for radio, and he always started with sharing the end first.

He would then take the next few minutes to tell "the rest of the story." I mean, the guy ended the segment with the actual phrase "and now you know the rest of the story!" and you could totally tell when he was chuckling. That he made himself laugh by drawing you in when the story was a silly one. It was infectious. He gave the punchline, the outcome, the end first. It's why people listened to the rest. Everyone always wanted to know how that ending came to be. It pulled them in.

It's why America loves Jeopardy! THEY GIVE YOU THE ANSWER. The challenge is asking the correct question. Among our population, in 2022, 15% of Americans watch "regularly" with 20% viewing "occasionally." We've been watching since 1964. And if you're like me, you get most of the questions wrong. ☺

Clearly this is an engaging strategy: tell the end first.

Keep the middle short.

The robust details in situations like short networking conversations almost never matter. Look for the opportune moment when you can tell your story; getting too deep into the details doesn't create clarity, nor is it useful. With today's short attention span you actually risk losing your audience because they don't have all the context and nuances. They weren't there. So, *most* of those details aren't as interesting as you might think.

Stick to the outcome in the beginning and a few impactful pieces of information that helped you achieve the outcome and the role you played. Tell enough of the journey to give "the rest of the story" and create clarity. What you share should be the bigger moments, the pivoting points, the events that made a difference. Telling a bit about the journey is what creates a feeling of genuineness that the listener wants, but too much and you risk talking at them, not with them. If who you are speaking to wants the details of a traditional "middle of the story," they will ask. This is where a real conversation begins to take place. If not, let them share and see if you can't find common ground elsewhere.

Make It Interesting

Stay on topic.

The few sentences you share after the punchline should be relevant. Be sure not to go off on a tangent or get too sidetracked. Remember, these are short snips of larger stories you can tell. Networking conversations are short and if one person talks too long it will disengage the rest, having the opposite effect. Keep the story tight, knowing the larger story can be told in a follow-up, or even better, when you get the opportunity to share it with a hiring manager or recruiter.

Use facts and metrics to support where possible.

First, I'm not suggesting you become a superior data analyst right away, or even at all. Although I'm sure the math teachers could! Here is an example to relay what I mean:

> *"I helped improve performance for my entire campus."*

You'll probably get a response from the person because they don't want to be rude, but you won't get the engagement you're looking for. Especially with a recruiter or on a phone screening (a phone screening is the conversation you have with another party and only if you pass their snuff test will it get you the coveted interview opportunity).

Instead try this:

> *"Campus test scores increased by 6% when I was on the assessment team."*

If you can't speak to this level of data (okay, then honestly what the heck is your district/campus doing with testing data???), I'm sure you know the impact on your classroom, so share that.

> *"My students improved by 11% and all campus test scores increased when I was on the assessment team."*

Full transparency, this is not how I thought when I was a teacher and job hunting but I wished I had known then what I know now. Taking the time while you're still in the classroom to practice thinking this way or gather this information while you still have an opportunity is amazing. Lean on your new growth mindset to develop the skill, fail, and try again.

Also, don't make these up. You either have the data or you don't. Keep searching until you find real data. And the more I personally learn about incremental improvements, the numbers are small. Now that I hire folks in my corporate roles, a huge red flag to dishonesty? Massive numbers. Change is hard and, to get better, change has to happen. If your class test scores improved 62%, Maury Povich might just show up out of nowhere and tell you that is a lie—because it almost always will be.

Building a Personal Brand and Telling a Story

notes

> Consider cause and effect...
> ...*but share it as an effect because of cause.*

This is a wonderful strategy if you are struggling with how to format your stories to share an outcome, especially in the beginning. Make it super easy for yourself—your "effect" is your outcome. The "cause" part makes up both the beginning of your story and the high-level journey. The middle should be brief. The details in the middle are great to share in a conversation and if who you are speaking with asks.

Pull Your Audience In

Laughter is good...

I'm putting this first to address the elephant in the room. I see this advice given a lot.

Want that guy/girl to fall in love with you? Make them laugh.

Want to break the ice? Make them laugh.

Want your significant other to stop being mad at you for a minute? *Try* to make them laugh.

Kid in a grumpy mood? You know what to say to get a smile. Especially when they don't want to!

Want your kid's little league team to gel? Tell a joke to make them laugh.

But here's the thing. Those aren't business relationships.

And almost every example is not one of a professional nature. Humor is so subjective. And when you're already nervous and anxious about a million other things, humor doesn't always come off how you intend. The problem with being "funny" and trying to make people laugh is that if they are not in the mood, don't like the topic you've chosen or who the butt of the joke is, or a litany of preconceived notions, you're sunk. Humor gets even more difficult to pull off without body language (phone or virtual) and missing tone (email and DMs).

I have been a paid subscriber to the Harvard Business Review for years. It has definitely upped my business acumen. But they even waffle on the helpfulness of humor in the workplace. In 2019, HBR published an article titled, "Making Jokes

During a Presentation **Helps Men But Hurts Women.**"[13] And then four years later in 2023, they published an article titled, "Research: Being Funny Can **Pay Off More for Women Than Men.**"[14]

Successful humor takes context. Successful humor requires a relationship with your audience.

This is a skill that can be learned and perfected. Just ask any standup comedian. But it takes a while and doesn't always work out. Just ask any standup comedian.

So, feel free to skip any "add laughter" advice you've heard, IMHO. Just be relaxed, at ease, not uptight. That alone, when sharing your brand online or in person for job opportunities, will get you much further.

...But good timing is better.

Instead of working to get a good laugh, tell an appropriate, interesting anecdote to affirm what others are saying. Have interesting information or something of note ready to share in order to jump into the conversation and participate. A story that begins with an outcome and includes a succinct but meaningful journey where you have appropriate pauses, interesting transitions, and good timing of a last sentence (...like Paul Harvey...) is the type of story most people enjoy hearing.

Draw on the five senses.

As humans, we like being able to relate to others in a way of our choosing. If you're looking to pull people in, rely on the five senses to make your story engaging. Consider how you can draw on people's five senses to relay your message, find common ground, and create a shared experience.

Consider any strong tie you have to a memory. I bet if you close your eyes, you can still see that sunset. You can smell that food—even taste how delicious it was. Or never forget the smell of that skunk. You can hear that singer like she was in the same room as you. You can feel that icy cold water, the sand in your toes, the warmth of the sun. Use the senses where you can as you share your story.

---

13 Jonathan Evans, Jerel Slaughter, Aleksander Ellis, and Jessi Rivin. "Making Jokes During a Presentation Helps Men But Hurts Women." Harvard Business Review, March 11, 2019, https://hbr.org/2019/03/making-jokes-during-a-presentation-helps-men-but-hurts-women. Accessed 22 December 2023.

14 Ella Miron-Spektor, Julia Bear, Emuna Eliav, Li Huang, Melanie Milovac, and Eric Yuge Lou. "Research: Being Funny Can Pay Off More for Women Than Men" Harvard Business Review, April 14, 2023, https://hbr.org/2023/04/research-being-funny-can-pay-off-more-for-women-than-men. Accessed 22 December 2023

Get Really, Really Good

For Pete's sake, stop procrastinating because you're recording yourself. This is a silly waste of precious time. People hear you talk every day and I bet 90% of the time you give ZERO practice before you speak. Ya just do it.

So, what is the problem with recording yourself when you're alone? If you don't, how do you expect to get better? Do you really want the first time you tell your story to be with a recruiter? Heck no. Make sure that swing-and-miss delivery is in front of your dog or your kid or your friend or you! Have them record you (well, your dog will make you do all the work) so you can get better.

Additional points to consider when you do begin practicing:

- Tone. It should match your personal brand.
- Be cognizant of filler words (ums, ands, likes, and any other hesitations or gap fillers).
- Read the transcript too. Writing a "script" as a starting point can help.
- Wean yourself from a script; don't let it become a crutch or make you sound robotic.
- Speak with confidence.
- Roleplay some Q&A. Have a friend ask you a question, or pretend you are asked a question, and respond.

The story you've begun to craft as you read the section above doesn't have to include everything suggested. Even better if over time you add tips and tricks from others via feedback. But be sure to at least consider all so that you are refining, making succinct, and crafting stories that are relatable and showcase you, your professional goals, and personal brand.

You'll notice that the last sentence also said "stories." That was on purpose. As you get better at telling and refining your story, you'll end up with several. This is even better because now you're prepared for multiple situations, different people/audiences, and varying scenarios. Over time, you'll have stories to explain:

- Why you left teaching
- The job/role you've now chosen or are pursuing
- Success
- Lessons learned
- What you want for your future and career path
- The drivers that motivate you

There will be more, and all will be able to articulate your personal brand and goals.

Now What?

So, after reading all that I hope you were constantly thinking how the information applies to you.

Developing what you can say, to whom, where and when, and how.

I hope you got excited when your brain finally connected a success story from your classroom into how you share it professionally via your brand. If not, that's okay. You're not getting out of it—it's the activity that goes with this chapter. ☺

1. Determine your personal brand. Use the checklist and tips provided earlier in this chapter. You can take notes below and list what you want to include.

2. Take inventory of your social media. Are you ok with what's public? Is that what you want a recruiter, your potential employer, your future team to see and know about you?
    - ✔ If you can say yes, great! Move on to item three.
    - ⊘ If not, take a few minutes to clean it up or flip your account settings to private.

Building a Personal Brand and Telling a Story

3. Use the framework ideas provided to craft a story. What can you say about choosing a new career? BONUS TIP: you can talk about financial freedom, but keep the language positive and don't harp on it. I know most of you are hurting for money or a more stable financial future, but focus on the other reasons and keep out any anecdotes that can seem like complaining. Just like the negotiation tip I shared in Chapter Three, bring up money, but save it for the end when you have a job offer in front of you. Telling your story to a hiring manager, recruiter, or to people at a networking event isn't a job offer. What can you say?

    a. You're ready for a new challenge.
    b. You feel bored with the scheduled monotony and want to diversify your day.
    c. You put in your time and are ready to help in a new way, solve a new challenge.
    d. If going after education-related jobs, maybe you want to scale your impact beyond your classroom walls.
    e. Perhaps you reflected, prayed, or meditated on it and felt called to something new.

4. Practice!! Ask those who care about you to listen and give you feedback.

8

LinkedIn, Resumes, Cover Letters, and References

This is a tough chapter for me. I really don't like that resumes are still "a thing." For even the most experienced executive, they are tough. I have had countless conversations and spent more hours of my life that have equated to weeks (goodness, I hope it's not actually months) on this silly document. Folks I've worked with in business who are REALLY, really good at what they do? They also struggle. When they begin looking for their next role, they also stress, second guess, type, delete, retype, and agonize.

Another reason I can't stand resumes is my personal bias. I have spent more time than I care to calculate writing, thinking on, and refining MY resume. And you know what?

> *I haven't gotten a job from applying online with a resume in my post-teacher career.*
>
> EVER.

notes

I've worked at five companies since leaving teaching. None from Monster.com or Indeed. None from "easy apply" via LinkedIn. None from applying directly to the company website. N.O.N.E. All five by referral, me calling on my network, meeting at an event, or what I've put on LinkedIn for recruiters to find me when they search.

Even crazier? This is true for my journey as a teacher. I moved a lot during my first marriage. Well, I still move a lot, so I can't blame the marriage entirely, but point being ONE time working on seven different campuses in five different school districts in a six-year period (you read that right)—ONLY ONCE did applying online get me an interview that led to a job. All the others were referrals and my network helping me get a job when I asked for their help.

> This is why I'm so serious about being able to tell your story and build a network.

We'll get deeper into networking and putting your storytelling to work in the next chapter.

In the end though? You still have to have a resume.

I'm also no expert on this subject. Most folks I know, especially at the middle of their career and executive level, hire a resume coach. They pay someone to document, create, and design their resumes. It's not cheap but it can be viewed as a cost of doing business if you seek senior, executive, and vice president roles. For you, though? Looking for early entry-level positions in a new career, you can absolutely do this, especially given the support here, from those around you, and the gobs of advice on the internet. You have everything you need, right now, to build a career-change-worthy resume.

I've put together a list of what I consider the best advice. Comprising what I've suggested to others and what they've shared about my resume in return. This list is a great starting point. There is no harm in Googling other tips or reading the blog or watching the vlog of a professional recruiter. All of it's good help, as long as you don't use research as an excuse to delay getting started.

I do recommend once you get a resume "done" (because let's be honest, it will never be) share it with your network (learn more in Chapter Nine). As you begin to meet folks at networking events, speak with recruiters, connect with folks at companies and in roles you want (what you read in Chapter Six), share your resume. Ask for feedback.

And because you're a teacher, you know that asking for generic feedback is not helpful just as receiving generic feedback is not helpful. You know that telling a student "Great job!" is a wasted moment. Telling them "Great job with your formatting. I can tell you put in more effort on this assignment and your source citation was correct" *is* helpful. Ask questions that are specific.

Don't ask these:

- 🚫 "Would you look at my resume?"
- 🚫 "What do you think about my resume?"
- 🚫 "Is my resume good?"

Ask these:

- ✔ "How does my bio compare to what you have on yours?"
- ✔ "Do the outcomes I described at XYZ job/role demonstrate driving change?"
- ✔ "Where is my leadership impact most prevalent?"
- ✔ "Where does my experience appear weak? Why?"
- ✔ "What stands out the most on my resume? Why?"
- ✔ "Aesthetically, what do you like/not like about the formatting?"
- ✔ "When you read my resume, what career/roles does it appear I am pursuing?"

The final bit before getting to what to add to your resume and how is to keep in mind the *purpose* of a resume:

> Get an interview by sharing in a succinct and meaningful way your achievements, experiences, and skills in the voice of your personal brand.

Want to see my very first resume when I tried to leave teaching?

I'm only showing because I know you won't laugh. I told you in Chapter Three I needed help!

ASHLEY PHILIPPS

123 Big Cat Cir. Lampe, MO 12345 · ashley@email.com · (123) 456-7890

SEEKING NEW POSITION

Self-motivated, goal driven, and enthusiastic prospective employee willing to do what it takes to meet customer needs to ensure company goals are met. Skilled in customer service, data analysis, curriculum development and design, and management to increase customer satisfaction and retention. Experience as a team leader and team member that is able to collaborate, problem solve, and build positive relationships with all stakeholders.

Skills and Qualifications

Leadership
- Plan, organize, and lead meetings to increase quality of instruction and test scores
- Model high quality classroom instruction and various teaching techniques
- Plan and lead staff Technology Summits to increase staff understanding and use of iPads and Google Education Suite (Forms, Docs, Sheets, Add-Ons).
- Communicate and collaborate with community business partners to increase relevance and work-ready potential employees upon graduation.

Technology
- PC, Mac/Apple, tablet/iPad, Microsoft Office Suite, Google Apps Suite, Internet, Blackboard/Moodle, Skype, SMART Board, Document Cameras, Flip Camera, Mobi, Edmodo Learning Platform, WikiSpaces, E-School/PowerSchool/Infinite Campus Student Learning Information Systems, and Social Media

Interpersonal
- Friendly, Team Member, Goal/Task Oriented, Strong Oral and Written Communication, Relationship Building/Conflict Resolution, and Professional Learning Communities

Adaptive
- Curriculum Development and Design, Backward Design/Objective Based Planning, Organized, Self-Motivated, Self-Manage, Flexible, Problem Solving, Prioritization, Quick Learner, Detail Oriented, and Driven

Education and Certifications

Master of Science in Education Curriculum & Instruction, Missouri Baptist University
Bachelor of Science in Education Social Studies, Southeast Missouri State University
Teacher Certificates: Social Studies, Business Education, Family/Consumer Sciences

ASHLEY PHILIPPS

123 Big Cat Cir. Lampe, MO 12345 · ashley@email.com · (123) 456-7890

Work History and Experience

CLASSROOM TEACHER, August 2008 – present
Listed School Districts Here- Combined all campuses into 1 experience

- Increased student test scores by 13% through implementation of Project Based Learning and Assessment *for* Learning.
- Increased campus World Geography test scores by 20% as team leader by collaborating and leading team members to create state objective-based lessons, activities, and assessments.
- Increased staff use of iPads and Google Forms 80% by leading three separate training and follow-up sessions for staff members.
- Daily responsibilities: student behavior management, communication with parents, collaboration with team and department members, daily instruction.
- Curriculum Development: World Geography, Pre Advanced Placement Geography, World History, and START Program
- Committee Member: Technology Integration, Strategic Planning - Curriculum, SchoolNet Assessment, Autism Team, AVID Site Team, Advanced Academics, Grade Policy, Assessment Data, Capturing Kid's Hearts Process Champion.
- Extra Duties: Assistant Coach for Girls' Lacrosse, Girl's Basketball, Softball, Volleyball, Senior Class Sponsor, Summer School

MARKETING/ADMINISTRATIVE ASSISTANT, March 2015 – present
RE/MAX

- On pace to complete $8 Million in sales this year
- Oral and written communication with prospective, current, and past clients
- Marketing: local and national press releases, social media, create and send paper and electronic marketing materials, utilize RE/MAX software (MainStreet, LeadStreet, Innovia, Paperless Pipeline)

SERVER, Seasonal Employment
Restaurant Name

- Responsible for customer satisfaction for all marina members and restaurant patrons
- Train new hires
- Manager of technology: MICROS Oracle System and tablet applications

---

Here is my current resume for reference as you look over the next few checklists. Take the same approach. How I bucketed my outcomes, you can make individual bullet points. That's fine! And yes, this is how I add my classroom teacher experience to my resume today.

ASHLEY M. PHILIPPS

email@mail.com · (123) 456-7890 · City, ST · LinkedIn

Helping others is what drives me. Whether I'm leading my team and coaching them through challenges or mentoring teachers and others through career pivots, I find I deliver my best work when I'm keeping someone else's success at the forefront. I'm a tenured leader who is looking for my next challenge in SaaS leading Revenue Enablement and Pre-Sales Solution teams.

Speaking Engagements & Publications

- "Positioning Enablement as a Strategic Function", GTM Buddy Voices of Enablement, Apr 2023
- "Career Transitions that Take Off", QuotaPath ValueProps Series, Season 2, Ep. 7, Feb 2023
- "Inspiring Woman in Enablement", SalesHood, Jan 2023
- "Onboarding Gets Everyone On Board", Selling Power Magazine, P. 19-22, Apr 2022
- "Data-Driven Enablement", SalesHood MULTIPLIERS Speaker, Oct 2022
- "The Seven Habits of Highly Effective [Sales] People", Loopio Loopicon Panel, Nov 2022
- "Top Female Sales Practitioners", SalesHacker, Aug 2020
- "Enablement Platform Demonstration", SalesHood MULTIPLIERS Speaker, May 2019
- "Sales Training is Only 1/3 of What You Need to Be Doing for Enablement", SalesHacker, Dec 2018
- "Quantifying Sales Learning Investments' Business Impact", Sales Force Productivity Conference, Oct 2018
- "Get Your Training Program Off the Ground", CallidusCloud C3 Customer Conf, Sept 2017

Professional Experience

Company Name   City, ST
VICE PRESIDENT, SOLUTION CENTER   April 2022 - Present
DIRECTOR, COMMERCIAL EFFECTIVENESS   May 2021 - March 2022

- 80% sellers hit quota, +40% pipeline increase via new RFx process, positive client NPS
- Projects: 2x Corporate rebrand, GTM of new SaaS solution, ~50 employees completed onboarding, design/launch Sales Associate Program, 5x developed job profiles & competency model per role
- Leadership: built and led Solution Center, Sales Associate program, RFx team, Solution Architects, and Enablement in one department, plus managed the Commercial tech ecosystem
- Enablement: Events (SKO), trade show certifications, role based GTM programs, Product Playbooks, coaching using personality and job profiles, asynchronous + vILT and ILT engagement, Methodology

Company Name   City, ST
PRINCIPAL SOLUTION CONSULTANT   March 2019- May 2021

- Top 3 largest deals in company history (ACV), largest license deal in company history, largest expansion in company history, and supported first $1M account
- ~$210k Avg. Enterprise Deal Size, ~$32k Avg. Growth Deal Size
- 15 days Time to First Deal, 74 Days Time to Second Deal, and Helped close 59 New Logos
- Designed and implemented customer-centric demos, built custom demos, ran clients Trials/POC
- Design and implement Enablement programs: Onboarding for Sales Directors and Solution Consultants, ran Partner Program, Sales Playbooks, and Competitive Intel

ASHLEY M. PHILIPPS
email@mail.com · (123) 456-7890 · City, ST · LinkedIn

Company Name [Tech Unicorn]   City, ST
SALES ENABLEMENT MANAGER   Feb 2018- Feb 2019
- Decreased ramp by 3 months (time to first deal), ~50% decrease in cost of onboarding new sales rep
- Created and implemented role based Competency Matrix for BDR, Sales, SE, CSM, plus bootcamps
- Events: Planned and executed Sales Kickoff FY 2019 (~75 attendees) and 3 QBRs in 2018
- Partnered with Product to design platform UI and AI/machine learning of pitch module

Company Name [Acquired by Company Name]   City, ST
SOLUTIONS MANAGER, PROFESSIONAL SERVICES   Oct 2016 - Jan 2018
- Closed $1M+ in SOW, top tier performer
- Supported 3 Enterprise and ~50 SMB reps to grow client base, revenue, and increase market share
- Leadership: 10 direct reports, 2 contractor relationships (6 people), worked directly with 75+ customers, supported cross-functional team of ~10 people to implement customers

Company Name [Acquired by Company Name]   City, ST
LMS PROGRAM MANAGER   Aug 2015 - Oct 2016
- Outcomes: over 95% adoption when launched new LMS: 86 departments, 15,000 employees
- Leadership: Managed 1 LMS Admin resource and 2 content developers
- Additional Highlights: Foundational training program, launch SaaS ticket system, curriculum design expert for all departments, assist in design/delivery of compliance for Ops, HR, and Legal

CLASSROOM TEACHER   Aug 2008 - Aug 2015
- 99% adoption of iPad program, 2x LMS launch to improve campus test scores and graduation rate
- x% increase in campus test scores, served on Curriculum and Assessment committees
- Implement project based learning, participate in cross-functional curriculum design at State level
- Leadership: Team Lead, Mentor, and a coach, 16x delivered peer professional development

Education & Certifications

Master of Science in Education Curriculum & Instruction, Missouri Baptist University
Bachelor of Science in Secondary Education, Southeast Missouri State University
Strategyn Jobs To Be Done Certification   ATD Sales Enablement Certificate
ATD Project Management for Learning Professionals Certificate

Revenue Ecosystem & Tech Expertise

Core Capability & CRM Platforms · O365, G-Suite, Okta, Adobe, Salesforce.com, Hub Spot
Enablement & Training Platforms · SalesHood, Guru, Litmos, Absorb
Engagement & Adoption Platforms · Salesloft, Outlook, Spekit, Pend.io
HCM & Collaboration Systems · Workday, SyncHR, ADP, Slack, monday.com, Trello, Asana
Business Intelligence & Legal · GoodData, PowerBI, IntelAgree, Docusign, HelloSign

notes

The Basics

- Be sure to have your full, legal name *and* a common/nickname (if applicable).
- Add contact info: area code + phone number, email, hyperlink your LinkedIn account.
- No need to add your full address, city and state will do.
  - If you live in a small town, you can put the closest, largest city (St. Louis, MO > Earth City, MO) or region (ex: Bay Area).
- Have a bio or career objective section.
  - Include what you want to do, what you desire in a next role and from your career, your overarching successes.
  - You can add your desire to change your career and any steps you've taken to make this happen and that you are ready.
  - Your bio can be flexible depending on what company, industry, or role you are seeking.
  - Have a few plug-and-play options to best fit the company or role you are sending your resume to.
- Add your college education (no need to add your GPA or high school).
- Add certifications, publications, and speaking engagements.
- List your experience; have your most current role first and sequential jobs after.
- If you received a promotion (team lead for example), be sure to point that out.
  - List the most important, current role first. On the line below, have your former title.
- Consider having a skills section, especially if your experience is or feels light.

Look and Feel

- Omit bubbly, script-style fonts.
- Almost all of your text should be black (aside from hyperlinks).
- You can make your name a large font and bold, but not too big (it's wasted space).
- Consider making your name and section headers a dark color but not black.
- Keep your bullet shape simple, you don't want them to distract (no emojis).
- Choose 11- or 10-point font. Any smaller is too small. Any larger appears juvenile.

notes

- Your picture—meh—add it if you like. It's on your LinkedIn profile and I'm not sure if this is the right thing just yet. It is becoming a more popular practice.
- Keep your resume to 1-2 pages (especially if you are short on experience).
- Some folks like having a banner on the left- or right-hand side for information (such as education and certifications). Aesthetically it can look interesting, but aside from that, too much overdesign makes it hard to decipher your resume and the recruiter will move on rather than giving it extra time.

Career Experience

- Be succinct. Most bullets should be one line; two lines is fine if it's a really impressive outcome and complex project.
- Get really succinct. Don't let 1-3 words take up an entire line.
- No fluff, no rambling. Get to the point and make each point bring value.
- Bullets that truly take up 3-4 lines of the page most likely should become two bullets.
- Be analytical; show the data (growth, change %, decrease waste, # improved).
- Ignore the fear or pressure of "Those who can't do, teach." It is nonsense.
- Write with confidence. Be proud of what you have accomplished. Believe in yourself.
- Your tone will come through in your writing so be positive about the entire task.

Add-Ons

- Trendy right now is a video introducing yourself, what you want from your career, and what makes you a great teammate. It's a great idea. Upload your video to your website, LinkedIn page, or Google Drive. Either hyperlink to it or use a QR code for access.
- Add logos (schools you graduated from, certifications).
- Hyperlink to something interesting (websites of programs you've completed is one idea or conferences you've attended or presented at).
- Consider having an online portfolio (a website of items related to the jobs you seek).
  - Going after a content, curriculum, or instructional designer role? 100% do this.

LinkedIn, Resumes, Cover Letters, and References

- Add snips, templates, and samples (I do not suggest giving it all away for free).
- Add videos of you at work (teaching, leading, sharing, presenting).
- Presentation decks (it is normal to "sanitize" information that may be proprietary but you had a large hand in. For example, you may pull the district/school name, info that identifies students, does not violate copyright laws of the program, but does show you using this information, applying it, designing it, and the impact YOU made using it, etc.).

How to Effectively Communicate Your Achievements

I have had this conversation quite a bit over the last few years, in conjunction with all the conversations I've had with teachers who want a career change. The post-COVID economy has been rough for a lot of folks, in all roles, in many industries. Writing this right now it seems like no one is immune to the down economy.

Most people get tripped up with trying to be succinct too soon in their writing process. You want immediate perfection or if you're like me, get annoyed at the time a resume takes and procrastinate while you mull it over in your mind for far too long. I advise you to ease up on yourself and just start writing. The first time you type out your bullets, type it however it comes out. There is no wrong way to do a first draft. And seriously—stop wasting time on formatting. Just document. Start with paper if that helps.

Write in the natural way humans communicate and share. It can be messy:

> *"I was this role this way, then did this, then this, added or changed this, and then this happened and then I got this as a result because of that."*
>
> *A more real example: "I taught seventh grade math for three sections in 2022 and I updated the Common Core lessons to include real-world scenarios so students could better relate to the content and grasp mathematical concepts and saw most students improve."*

Once you free-form documented and have exhausted everything you can think of about that role or job, then refine the bullet points. Cut out 30-40% of the words. I know that sounds like a lot, but my guess is, if you wrote free form and had an idea dump, there is plenty that does not help succinctly tell the outcome, your direct impact, or why what you did matters. Also, if your statement lacks data, go crunch some numbers in your gradebook and look at pre- and post-assessment performances or pass/fail rates.

Refining will come out something like this:

"Did this, specifically this way, and achieved the result."

A more real example:

Developed relatable math-based scenarios for grade 7 Common Core math resulting in 17% increase in class pass rates.

Now, flip it and make it as succinct as possible while still making sense:

"Result because of this, this way."

A more real example:

17% increase in pass rates of math curriculum by adding real-world scenarios.

Continuing to refine. You have now made your resume bullet points outcome first, not verb first.

Adding dates in your bullet points? You did that at the start when you listed the job.

Adding in grade level? Meh. Not relevant and chances are you put it in your job title when you said you were a 6th and 7th grade math teacher at ABC School. However, you can keep the grade if your job title leaves it out and you think it helps tell your story.

Adding in too much teacher jargon? You'll lose your audience, and it doesn't matter. You can leave out a lot of the program tiles and such in bullet points. Now, if you're certified in a program, that goes in your education section.

Why the push to be so tight on your words and put the outcome first? People stop reading very quickly, within the first few sentences (think books, blogs, articles...think about how many times you actually finish reading a post, an article). Recruiters and hiring managers are no different. With resumes you have seconds to get your point across.

Here are a couple of examples I gave to two different people in my network. One is a teacher wanting to start a new career, one to a peer already in the corporate world.

LinkedIn, Resumes, Cover Letters, and References

notes

> **Here are two typical bullet points:**
>
> - Maintained a pass rate for 6th grade students 25% higher than average for the 2022/2023 school year.
> - Designed and led changes in channel strategy, sales structure, segmentation, new business acquisition and role specialization approaches across the organization accelerating revenue growth, increasing YOY New Business by $15.2M while creating $7.1M in annual operational savings.
>
> **I suggested:**
>
> - 25% increase in pass rates for 6th grade students.
>
> - $15.2M increase YOY New Business, + $7.1M in annual operational savings via strategy for channel, sales structure segments, role specialization, and new business acquisition.

Keep in mind, your resume does not have to tell ALL the details. It should be engaging enough to make the reader lean in and want more. They should want to ask you HOW you accomplished these successes and how you can do it at their company. That's the interview.

My last bit on the resume itself is to approach it the same way you did crafting your story in the last chapter. Write a really great generic version. Know it well. Then when you see a role that you desire and plan to apply for, update your resume to create a company, role-specific version. Trust me, you will want to do this. I know it's work and uploading the same version is easy. It's also, dare I say…lazy.

Moreover, AI has been in HR software looooong before you heard about ChatGPT in 2022. Applicant tracking software, or ATS, is hiring software that almost every company purchases directly or uses indirectly by contracting a firm to do it on their behalf. ATS will scan your resume. If you don't customize your resume and not enough of the words in the company's job description/posting match, your resume will be rejected and never even be seen by human eyes. Even when you customize it, it may not be enough for the online portal uploads. Yup. It happens. This is 100% Indeed, Monster.com, and corporate website uploads style scanning and it will almost always, 99% of the time, lead to nothing. It will kick you out every time because as a teacher-heavy resume you won't have enough job history in the field. Online listings are not transition-teacher friendly.

Another thing ATS programs don't like are non-traditional, busy resumes. Later in the chapter, the exercise includes addressing writing and updating your resume.

Canva is a very cool product that has beautiful templates and layouts. Be careful, though, because unless you are giving that beautiful version to a human, the online upload won't like it. Consider having an upload version that is black and white, traditional format text as well as a more engaging and visually stimulating version you can email and share with people. The content can be the same, it's the formatting that may cause issues.

So, create a bomb.com resume and have bios to plug and play. Tweak the bullet points and use language found in the job description before uploading and sharing to specific jobs. Again, yes, this stinks because it takes time; however, it's a low brain-power lift because you're not making it up. Pull words and phrases directly from the job description. Have THIS version ready to send to a human after and during your outreach. In the next chapter, we'll talk about outreach to people about the job you want BEFORE you apply at all.

Cover Letters

I had one (have one). Used it on the online upload circus for online job hunting all those years ago. It never helped me, and I haven't used it since. But here is what I will say. Have one anyway. If a company has antiquated hiring practices (and this is most of them) this is a step in the process. Even if no one reads it. I am not kidding. Even today when I hire someone, a resume ends up being sent after conversations and uploaded into the HR software when I know I'm ready to make a job offer. It would be senseless to disqualify yourself from a role over something so silly and easy to have ready to share.

Keep it to one page. Personally, I believe adding all the old school names and addresses of yourself and who the letter is to with crazy spacing like I was taught in my business class in middle school is overkill. Address it to the hiring team. Then get to the body of the letter.

Make the cover letter be about the journey. Write it in your professional voice. In case it is read, make sure it is engaging. If you do this right, it can/will help articulate your career transition in case you can't get an audience with someone at a networking event or phone call. It is a piece of content to tell your story.

Here is an example. My cover letter is SO OLD, so with permission, here is one from a teacher I've recently mentored.

Christie

January 23, 2024

Dear Hiring Manager,

As an experienced ▓▓ LMS user and developer, I have spent 13+ years refining my capabilities and integrating SaaS (25-50% of content) to create dynamic online learning experiences for 6th-8th graders in 6+ courses. My middle school students saw 20+% increase in pass rates with some increasing nearly 65%. As a leader in my company, I am charged with the Professional Learning of 20+ faculty and am part of a program that profited over $6 million dollars in the 22-23 fiscal year.

For most of my teaching career I have been a part of alternative education: long-term suspension and online learning. ▓▓ has helped me create greater access to quality course content. As a long-term suspension teacher, I was responsible for teaching all course offerings 9-12. Starting in the early 2010s, I taught myself ▓▓ to build self-paced courses to meet diverse curricular needs and help at-risk students find a path to graduation. Now, ▓▓ is literally my classroom, building a community of middle schoolers learning at home all over the state of ▓▓ from cities to rural communities in over 380 districts. Furthermore, I am a highly requested teacher due to my ability to form positive relationships and dynamic presentation style.

▓▓ is a company dedicated to product improvement, new ideas, simplicity, respect, and accountability. This vision directly correlates to my own personal and professional goals of continuous improvement. I take great ownership in my product both in what I produce as a teacher and the courses I write as a creator. I am never quite satisfied with the status quo and am always looking for ways to better my skills and my product. I believe my technical knowledge, communication skills, and desire to help others achieve their vision and goals make me well-suited for a Solutions Engineer role.

Please contact me at ▓▓ or ▓▓ if you have any questions. I look forward to sharing more about how I can be a valuable asset to the ▓▓ community.

Best Regards,

Christie

notes

Same advice for writing this as I gave for crafting your story since this is simply a written version. Use all that great work you did crafting your brand and story for this.

- Keep it on brand.
- Paragraph One—tell outcomes and success stories that relate specifically to the job you want or are applying for.
- Paragraph Two—Share who you are, tell the career change journey succinctly and focus on the positive reasons you desire a new career; keep the "middle" sparse.
- Paragraph Three—Tell why YOU are the fit for their company or team. Refer to the research you have done about the company and give specific examples (don't be generic).

Update (or Create) Your LinkedIn Profile

In Chapter Nine we'll talk more about how you will use your LinkedIn page to connect and network with others. You should take time to continually refine it. Far more people will see your LinkedIn page than your resume or cover letter.

Like it or not, social media is HUGE in the networking world
If you don't have a LinkedIn, create one then address the items below

1. Is your picture of YOU only, clear, *and recent*?
2. Update your banner – I prefer personal image, not corporate
3. Tagline – about you, your personal brand – NOT your "job"
4. Update your About section – mix of personal, career, and desired future
5. Are your Experience, Education, Licenses & Certification, and Skills updated? If not, update them
6. Add or update Volunteer, Interests, and Causes
7. Do you have any Recommendations? If not, look at mine or a peer who does and jot down ideas of WHO you can ask and WHY from that person (you don't need to ask just yet...)

LinkedIn, Resumes, Cover Letters, and References

notes

Choose a banner that is personal, yet professional. It can be a conversation starter. For example, mine is an image of a sunset at one of my favorite family vacation spots. I know exactly where it is. I was on the beach in Destin, FL near the Blue Surf Condominiums we stayed at when I was a girl. The picture makes me happy and feel at ease. Now, if I'm asked about the photo, it's easy to tell the story and talk. And not only is it a specific spot that I love, it is of a sunset. Sunset is my favorite time of day at the beach. I'm the most relaxed, it means I've spent the day lounging, the beauty is incredible, and it means another day full of new opportunities is coming my way very soon.

Update your About section to reflect your cover letter and your career transition. This is big online real estate. You can share where you've been, where you want to go, your achievements, and why YOU might just be who they are looking for. All the work you did to craft your personal brand and cover letter should make this pretty easy. Include your successes, and of course, keep it succinct. People don't finish reading paragraphs so anything too lengthy (basically anything after the "see more" prompt) probably won't be read, much less ever viewed.

Make your Experience section reflect your resume. Here is where you can put the bullets of outcomes you drove and committee time that fits more with corporate roles you seek. Also, you do not need to put the exact school district or campus. I bundled all my teaching experience into one role and had bullet points from all my schools as if it were one. You may consider leaving yours separate if you don't have other jobs and you want to show the time you've been employed.

You can pull out your committee work and work outside the classroom and list them as their own experiences. Rember, the section is Experiences, not Jobs. This way you can show flexibility and increased experience, and be more articulate about your leadership, about your role, and about the outcomes you contributed to.

Update your skills to match the skills on your resume. Add volunteer work. And lastly, add those various certifications (especially ones that transfer as a non-classroom teacher).

Taking LinkedIn to the Next Level

LinkedIn will be the most common way you leave a networking moment and know to find the person later. Email is probably right at the top too, but LinkedIn is where you can learn more about your new connection prior to sending an email. To prepare to send direct messages (DMs) and connection requests we'll need to identify good fits, not just any fit. Influencers and gossip have made us feel we need high numbers of online connections to be validated. That somehow volume equates to reality. I guess if your goal is selling shampoo via a collab from Cool and Trendy Salon that would be true. However, that could not be less true for career networking. I'll take one quality connection over twenty unrelated connections all day, every day.

Taking your LinkedIn to the next level means updating or doing the following. If you're unfamiliar with LinkedIn, leverage their help site.

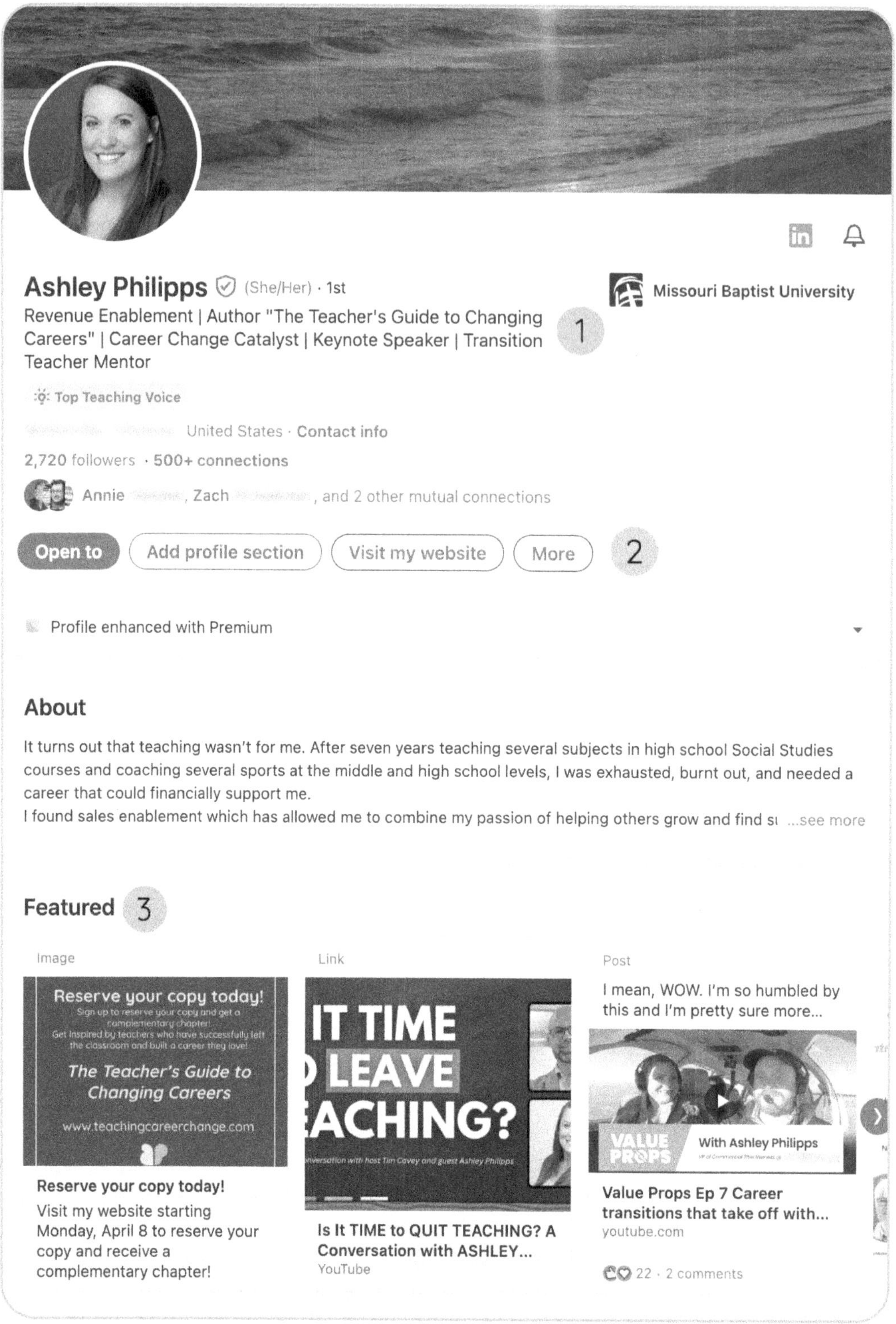

Ashley Philipps ✓ (She/Her) · 1st   Missouri Baptist University
Revenue Enablement | Author "The Teacher's Guide to Changing Careers" | Career Change Catalyst | Keynote Speaker | Transition Teacher Mentor

💡 Top Teaching Voice

United States · Contact info
2,720 followers · 500+ connections

Annie _____, Zach _____, and 2 other mutual connections

[Open to] [Add profile section] [Visit my website] [More]

Profile enhanced with Premium

About

It turns out that teaching wasn't for me. After seven years teaching several subjects in high school Social Studies courses and coaching several sports at the middle and high school levels, I was exhausted, burnt out, and needed a career that could financially support me.
I found sales enablement which has allowed me to combine my passion of helping others grow and find s... ...see more

Featured

Image

Reserve your copy today!
Sign up to reserve your copy and get a complementary chapter.
Get inspired by teachers who have successfully left the classroom and built a career they love!

The Teacher's Guide to Changing Careers

www.teachingcareerchange.com

Reserve your copy today!
Visit my website starting Monday, April 8 to reserve your copy and receive a complementary chapter!

Link

IT TIME LEAVE ACHING?

Is It TIME to QUIT TEACHING? A Conversation with ASHLEY...
YouTube

Post

I mean, WOW. I'm so humbled by this and I'm pretty sure more...

VALUE PROPS With Ashley Philipps

Value Props Ep 7 Career transitions that take off with...
youtube.com

💬 22 · 2 comments

Skills 4

Team Leadership

👥 13 endorsements

(Endorse)

Learning Management Systems

👥 11 endorsements

(Endorse)

Show all 9 skills →

Recommendations 5   (Recommend Ashley)

Received   Given

Kiran ~~~~~~~ 🔗 · 2nd
Corporate Strategy | Strategic Alliance | Cloud
January 31, 2020, Kiran worked with Ashley but they were at different companies

Ashley was my contact at CallidusCloud for all the PS work we did. She was extremely helpful with communicating and eliciting requirements clearly. She was able to help set up a successful PS delivery partnership with RapidValue. I would definitely recommend her any day for her PM capabilities !

Dan ~~~~~~~ 🔗 · 2nd
Enterprise Sales I Automating Taxes for the Internet Economy
November 6, 2018, Dan worked with Ashley but on different teams

Ashley is a great colleague. From creating an initial onboarding/bootcamp for new hires to working alongside prospects she is always there to help. She is responsive on any questions I have and very proactive in helping the sales team with anything we need to move deals forward. The training programs she has set up at MindTickle have been some of the best I've had. She is fun to work with, smart and goes above and beyond what she is asked.

Show all 4 received →

notes

1 Headline

This is ***invaluable real estate*** on your profile page. Why? It's how folks find you when they don't know you.

When a recruiter (or anyone) does a search for a role they need filled they use what is referred to as "keywords," meaning terms that describe the skills, experience, and role-related tasks they will need a person to do.

There is a possibility that some firms/recruiters pay for expanded search capabilities, but this is not the majority (If you're curious, it's how LinkedIn makes money. Your profile is free, but if firms and companies want to deep search the database of profiles? Paid).

However, don't count on additional spend being how a large majority of your known and unknown network can find you.

> Search returns come from keywords used that match your headline.

Did you write an immense amount in the "About" section? Irrelevant…

Did you spend months refining the proof points for each of your "Experiences"? Wasted time…

Did you spend weeks adding details of a major project? Too bad…

UNLESS your headline is a succinct snip of your personal brand and the career path and next role you desire, you won't be found and all that hard work on your profile won't get noticed.

Ensure your headline is on point. All the other page efforts absolutely become worth it.

> **Still want more tips? Google "LinkedIn Headline" tips.**

2 "Open To"

This one is a bit slippery as usage of and message of it begets mixed signals.

The original intent is stellar. It came about during the COVID-19 pandemic when the economy went bonkers. Layoffs in the thousands while the industry next door hired just as fast. Then these same companies flipped six months later. New hires months into a role, let go on a Friday. Companies that whiplash reacted to a down market found they let too many resources go and then were frantic to bring folks back.

"Open to" was meant to quell the madness and let the market know you were in search of connections, conversations, and new roles. The premise was that you would click the radio button and a banner would appear on your profile image that said #OpenToWork if you were in search of a job and if you were hiring, it would add #Hiring to your profile image. This was meant to improve job matchmaking.

Somewhere along the way, the layoffs lasted too long. The shake-up wasn't quelled, and the economy did not rebound.

Now, there is mixed views of #OpenToWork being on your profile too long (or at all), or that it has negative connotations (not skilled enough, lacks something, not as strong as...). From what I've read, some give pause and would say, unfairly, 'there is a reason they are available...'

I don't know how to steer you in the right direction here other than to say, you know you and this decision will not end or be the reason you don't reach your ultimate career goals.

Personally, I've read about the debate. My reaction? If a company sees #OpenToWork as a reason NOT to interview you or consider you, that is a red flag and a solid indication of the company culture. Not a problem with you.

I'll ask this: would you want to work for a company that judges you negatively based on using a tool the way it is designed on a networking platform?

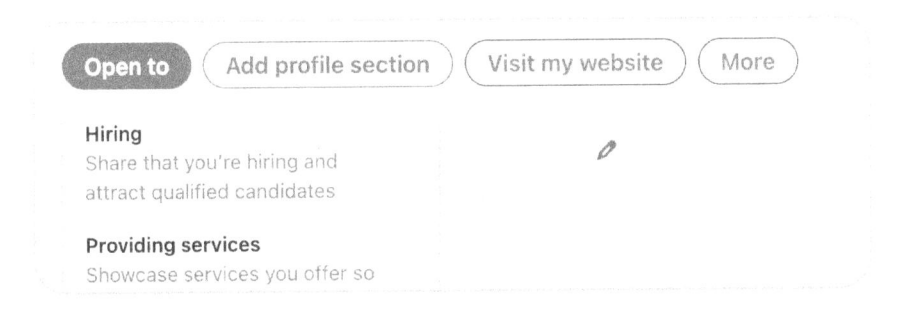

LinkedIn, Resumes, Cover Letters, and References

notes

3 Featured Posts

Think of this section of your page as a highlight portfolio with commentary. Here's how Featured Posts works:

You write a post on LinkedIn—no, really, you'll actually need to do this—write posts. 😬 😖 😐

Write about what you know:

Write about best practices in classroom behavior management.

Write about curriculum or lesson plans.

Write about test and assessment bias.

Write about what you have strong opinions and solutions about.

Write about driving students to performance outcomes and what makes you great, successful, or how you learned to do this the hard way.

Start to make posts that marry your teaching experience to the new career and role you seek (this would be exceptionally similar to writing about your time investments from Chapter 4: Don't Say No" and starting to use jargon and flex your growing business acumen from Chapter 5).

We're not going to post and delete.

We're also not going to get down on not meeting a high expectation of engagement/comment...that only you know about and made up.

Engagement comes with time. I'm not going to get into it here, but the LinkedIn algorithm is a beast and plays a huge role in who sees your content. I stopped paying for LinkedIn and my engagement dropped. So what. I'd rather save the money than get a few thumbs ups.

Practice sharing your stories and your successes to help you get a job. That is the goal and why you spend time doing this, not popularity.

Once you consistently make posts, people will engage. More engagement comes from people knowing you (aka your network) and wanting to support you. They can like and react as well as make comments.

Once a post becomes the least bit popular and has more engagement or interaction than your other posts, Feature it.

notes

2 ways:

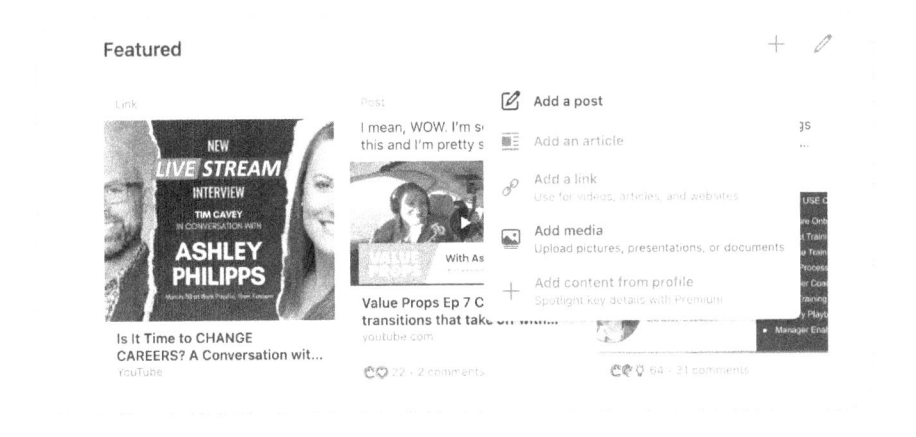

4 Recommendations

I touch on this as a quick fill-in as you develop your job references. It's in the section below.

Simply take time to identify who can write you a recommendation. Then in your note to request, include:

- A greeting
- What you need (a recommendation)
- A request for specific projects or stories
- Why you chose them

notes

- What you achieved together
- Thank you

Keep in mind, those that give to others will get back what's meant to be. Consider writing recommendations before you start asking for others to write them for you.

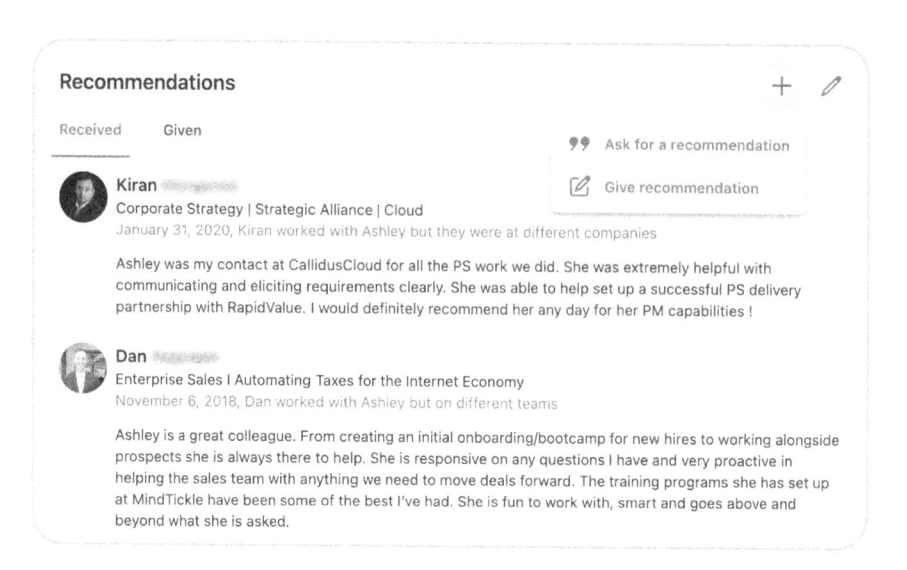

> **Recommendations**
>
> Received Given
>
> **Kiran**
> Corporate Strategy | Strategic Alliance | Cloud
> January 31, 2020, Kiran worked with Ashley but they were at different companies
>
> Ashley was my contact at CallidusCloud for all the PS work we did. She was extremely helpful with communicating and eliciting requirements clearly. She was able to help set up a successful PS delivery partnership with RapidValue. I would definitely recommend her any day for her PM capabilities!
>
> **Dan**
> Enterprise Sales I Automating Taxes for the Internet Economy
> November 6, 2018, Dan worked with Ashley but on different teams
>
> Ashley is a great colleague. From creating an initial onboarding/bootcamp for new hires to working alongside prospects she is always there to help. She is responsive on any questions I have and very proactive in helping the sales team with anything we need to move deals forward. The training programs she has set up at MindTickle have been some of the best I've had. She is fun to work with, smart and goes above and beyond what she is asked.
>
> Ask for a recommendation
> Give recommendation

5 Skills

This is another area of your profile where you can highlight strengths.

There are I-don't-even-know-how-many-skills listed in the picklist for this section. You don't type into it what you want it to say, rather you add from a list provided to you.

My tip here is, less is more and add what matters to the role you seek. If you have (like I did when I first started using LinkedIn and for way too long after) 30, 40+ that's too many. I know firsthand that you'll be listing too many for the role you want.

For example, if you're going after a CSM role at an EdTech company, it's assumed you're experienced in Microsoft Office. You can do the basics. There is no need to add rote skills. The flip side is if you do list items like this, it can work against you and appear you lack skills so you're "padding your list," if you will.

notes

As you network with people who understand your skillset, they can learn, based on interactions with you, from stories, and knowing firsthand, that you are proficient at said skill. They can "endorse" you.

I can't say in my career this played a large role or even had a role at all in my journey. What I do want you to understand is why it exists and that it will help someone get to know you better during this journey if you're looking for a way to highlight skills you have that match the role you want.

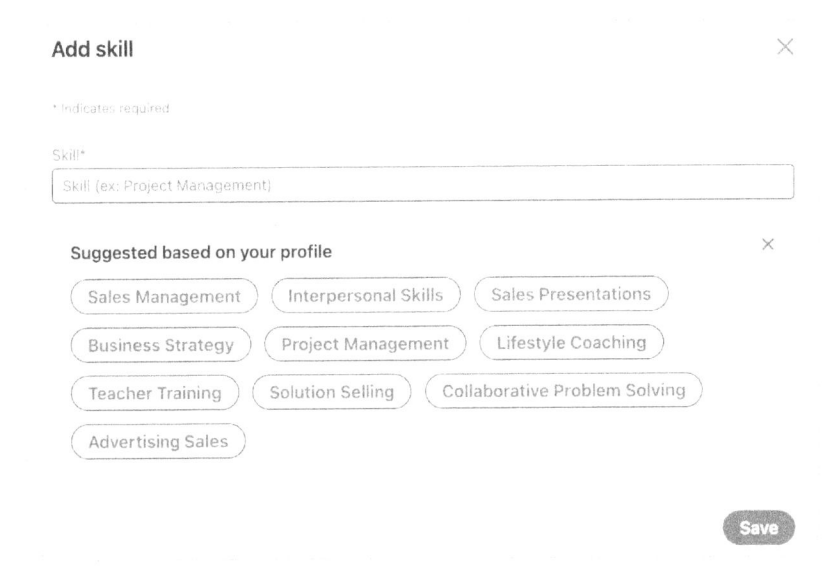

Add skill   ✕

*Indicates required

Skill*

[Skill (ex: Project Management)]

Suggested based on your profile   ✕

(Sales Management)   (Interpersonal Skills)   (Sales Presentations)

(Business Strategy)   (Project Management)   (Lifestyle Coaching)

(Teacher Training)   (Solution Selling)   (Collaborative Problem Solving)

(Advertising Sales)

[Save]

Once your LinkedIn profile is in a better place, put it to work. Over time your LinkedIn page can become a time taker, just like a resume, and you find yourself making tweaks where one isn't needed or spending time to make such a small impact that it wasn't worth the time spent.

References

I used to think "sharing my references" simply meant me giving a prospective company a list of people who would tell said company I was a good person, that they liked me and thought/assumed I did good work. I was wrong. References are strategic and you should use them as such.

I cannot stress enough that you should have several, depending on the job opportunities associated with needing a reference, and it should include

notes

people with various levels of relational experience to you. Meaning, have references that are:

- Acquaintances and can speak to your character,
- References who reported to you (formally or informally) at a peer level and if they were a direct report to you,
- Someone who was a direct manager of yours, and
- A skip-level/higher-level leader you and your team reported to.

Prep them. It is your responsibility to coach them. They should know what job you are applying for at what company, stories to share about you, and what you specifically need them to talk about relative to the job and skills. Prepping is not cheating, prepping is smart. I'm not kidding—you need to outright know what they will say about you. They can share their own stories, that's authentic. Nothing needs to be scripted word for word, but you should roleplay and discuss this.

A cautionary tale if you don't:

I'm going to call this associate principal I reported to Jim Toney. Jim was a fan of mine. He liked my work, how I ran my classroom (We were in the "tight ship" guild. Definitely a no-nonsense vibe in the classroom.) I asked him to be a reference for me. He gladly accepted. I gave the prospective company his name and email address.

Then he got the email to be my reference for my first job leaving teaching (as you recall, I resigned on the third day of students on campus). I called him to make sure he booked a time to talk with the company (the email was to schedule time with someone in their HR department). Shockingly, he was an a**hole. He was pissed that the job wasn't another classroom job. He didn't go through with being my reference. At the time I was mad. I didn't have a lot of options and he just bails? It was probably for the best. Actually, I know it was. I'm feeling grateful as I write this out because if he would have said to that prospective company what he said to me? No way I'd have gotten an offer. Heed my warning, prep and KNOW you'll be represented in a favorable light.

But what if you don't want your school to know you're looking to leave? The principal is out. So is the team/department lead and the counselors. Definitely most of your peers. Let me put your mind at ease—people who want to leave their current job are also in this tight spot.

Do this.

Remember how you've joined a meaningful committee or activity while teaching for your next role? Good, me too. Have someone from the committee write a LinkedIn recommendation or a written, letter-style recommendation for you. Those are authentic, are meant to be reflective of projects, and they should not signal to anyone on campus you're looking to leave. For all the other committee members and leaders know, you're wanting a promotion in the field of education or you're planning to apply to get your master's degree. You have principal aspirations. Whatever the motivation is, it shouldn't even matter. If you did great work building a relationship with this person, and helped make the project a success, there should be zero hesitation to complete one on your behalf.

You do still need references, though.

- That's where volunteer work or work outside of the classroom comes into play. These folks can be critical.
- Past leaders who support you and will vouch for you without telling your current boss.
- Trusted, close-knit relationships at school can work well. Just be sure they value your future as much as you do.

Now What?

Complete the following checklist:

- Create or update your resume. Use the checklists provided in the chapter. Then refine your resume.
    - Need a template? There are some good free ones online.
    - Canva has some great free templates for the email version you create.
- Write a cover letter following the format provided. A Word doc is sufficient.
- Update your LinkedIn profile.
    - Be sure it matches your resume and cover letter and makes your personal brand shine.
- Compile a list of potential references and make notes of what they can share about you to help you get your next job.
- Call your potential references. Let them know you're looking and ask if they are open to being a reference.
    - If they say no, move on to the next.
    - If they say yes (and I'm sure they will), prep them and give them an idea of your timeline. Be sure to let them know you'll certainly be in touch before a company calls them down the line.

9

Networking, Outreach, and Interviews

We're close to the end now. After reading, planning, and completing the exercises it probably feels like May 4th of a school year. You're tired (Exhausted? Drained? Anxious? Elated?), but so, so close to another end. We've covered a lot. We've discussed overcoming fears and being anxious in this decision to leave the classroom, assessed your values, strengths and opportunities, sorted through a good choice as a next step versus going after anything and everything, and worked to pursue a role, a company you can get behind and use to build some career longevity.

You have an updated LinkedIn page, resume, cover letter, and you are working on references.

This feels like a good place to pause, reiterate, and appreciate:

> **Yes, it is HARD to change your career path, but it is not impossible** *and it is 1M% worth every effort you make.*
>
> *It is going to positively change your life.*
>
> **What is ACTUALLY HARD is waking up every day to do a job you loathe (dare I say, hate?) and be responsible for the education of a young person.**
>
> *We spend far too many hours working to stay where we are—unhappy, unfulfilled, and financially strapped.*
>
> *Everyone deserves better.*

notes

Now, at the end of this book, you have everything you need to make it real:

- A clear vision for your next career.
- Jobs, industries, and companies that interest you.
- Roles you can see yourself doing, stick with, and build a career on.
- Transferable skills that are for a corporate setting, not just a classroom.
- A personal brand.
- The ability to tell your story (confidently!).
- An updated LinkedIn profile.
- New or updated resume, cover letter, and references.

Time to pull it all together and put it to work. This last chapter of guided instruction is all about going and doing.

- Network for real connections, the right connections.
- Outreach to your network, recruiters, and hiring managers.
- Interview tips and preparation.

> And doing it in this order matters.

Networking

Like my friend Tracey reminded me, networking is hard for teachers because when you're a teacher, your entire world is other teachers. Coupled with that is the idea, "I don't belong here because *I'm just a teacher*," that is so strong in us teachers. Like, The Force strong—except it's evil like The Empire. I blame that nasty, way-too-common adage: *those who can't do, teach*. UGH. Overcome these feelings by leaning on a growth mindset and tell yourself:

> I do belong here because I am a talented professional.

More truths about me: remember I had imposter syndrome at that first job at the solar company? This feeling followed me for years. I can't say I have regret, because I believe my journey happened exactly as it should have, but my goodness it was such a waste of my mental space, impeding accelerated growth. This nagging feeling of inferiority stuck around for the first two and a half years. It feels unreal looking back now because I believe so differently after living, learning, and mentoring others.

I also mentioned I wanted out of the sales tool company so, so badly. That was my aha moment, my kick in the pants to go to more networking events to vet a company and decide IF I even wanted to work there. I had to at this time, no one was going to "save me." My environment was different. Rory bailed me out of a layoff. A recruiter bailed me out of an underpaid job that felt like an imminent layoff. I had no plan to get the next job. I was still wallowing around and felt almost as lost as my original job search. Applying online was not working. Once again, I felt stuck.

I decided to be bold. After years doing semi-related work in learning software and being in training departments, I realized the market of sales enablement was a pretty good match for me. My strengths, what I valued, and the number of available opportunities were a fit. I'm still in this field today. Ashley of Careers Past may have learned about enablement earlier if I had been able to give myself the advice I can now provide in this book, but I had no guidebook. So, I went to an in-person event specifically for enablement professionals (You should do this too. Whatever your interests were from Chapters Five and Six, go to events about that. Find one to go to now. Don't wait.). Once I got there, I participated. I got out of my own head and calmed myself by breathing while I listened to the presentation. Because it was a networking event, there were activities for us to participate in. That also made it easier to have something to focus on *doing* rather than focus on jittery nerves. I felt my skills were lacking. I didn't have the stories of others. I didn't have the experience of others. I certainly didn't have the resume to match the room. But I still participated.

What I didn't realize was how bold I was. This networking event was hosted by a direct competitor of my current company! That I honestly did not know when I showed up. C'est la vie.

It did become clearer where I had inserted myself, and I got scared and I tried to bounce early. The group exercise and discussion portion were over and it was time to mingle. As I made my way out via the back of the room, scooting to the door, Elay intercepted my exit. I'll never forget it. I wonder if I was visibly sweating. Probably.

But he looked me in the eye, said "hi, I'm Elay" and stuck out his hand for a shake. I took his hand; I think I said my name. A thing about Elay, he has a thoughtful look about him when some new information intrigues him. He tilts his head a certain

notes

way and his eyes slightly squint. It is a look that means he is actively listening. I became familiar once we worked together. At the time I thought, "someone help me, this guy knows I'm an imposter!" But it was real, genuine curiosity about who I was and why I was there, and he outright said we should talk.

I left that building on Main Street in the FiDi of San Francisco freaking floating on air. I didn't even notice the horrible smell of BART as I rode the train back to Oakland. I emailed him that night. Within days I was at their office at the convergence of Pacific and Columbia Streets having a conversation about my career. It wasn't a "job interview." At least not in the traditional sense and what I had been used to. Elay wanted to get to know me, what I wanted. We sat in comfortable seating in a relaxed, open area of the office, not across from one another in a big, stuffy conference room or an office. I thought it was great. I had never had a conversation like this, this way, with this type of audience, with this much potential. I told him I had been a teacher, that I was fumbling around in tech with no direction, and I was afraid my resume didn't tell a story. My friend Larkin was the one to point out this real concern of her path when we worked together. It resonated with me; it was me too. Of course, I was more guarded in this message and more confident about my experience in the moment, but it was in the back of my mind. I even told him about this book—that's how long this baby has been cookin' in my brain!

Of course he had a role, a gap he needed to fill, but he presented it in a way that fit what I could do now, and it gave me room for growth. When I wrote earlier in this book to put real effort into finding out what you can about company culture, my time at this company is why. It took me accepting three jobs of what was put in front of me, thinking I didn't have a choice, zero negotiation, having none of them work out or leave me feeling valued, to understand the importance of company culture and finding where you are a good fit.

When you do go to networking events, look for people related to where you want to be. Find people that have similar roles, want to take the same path as you, have ideas to share, and are in the same or similar industries of interest. Find people that are currently doing or have done what you want to be doing. Don't get me wrong. Be open and kind. Meet a lot of people. It will be so much more fun. But put in the effort to connect and network with people who can help you, and you them, when it comes to your careers.

Once you exchange info, be it phone, email, or LinkedIn—keep in touch, really. Don't just say you will, actually do it. At least most of the time. Once people get to know you, they will remember you. And then when an opportunity comes up and they are asked, "Hey, we need help with XYZ. Know anyone?," you will come to mind because you are kind, gave your time and effort, and told your authentic story. You connected with this person and stayed in touch. You may not even be an exact fit for the role, but they will think of you. And that's good! Because that intro will either help get you the open role which you can grow into or may open the door to a different opportunity. The best employees have soft skills. Hard skills/job skills can be learned. But relationships? Those are key and take time. And teachers are really good at this. And most folks can't fake it for long. Ignore the ones who have successfully slipped through the cracks. These people are wildly outnumbered and even if it's not openly discussed or called out, people know. Best not to spend your time getting stuck here.

Give purposeful networking a go. Even now on your school campus and at networking opportunities. Be the person who is seen. Not in an annoying way, but in a way that shows genuine curiosity about those around you. Put yourself out there and make new friends and acquaintances because it feels good. From here you'll start to build a support network for your career.

But what if I'm just too nervous? Anxious? Can't see myself there?

I feel anxious a lot. I always have. When I moved to California for my career, I had to get over it. You have to get over it. *You've got to*. It's hard. Really hard, but put yourself out there. This is me giving you tough love. Practice breathing techniques to calm yourself. Because the open secret is, **everyone is a bit anxious at an event**. *Very few people are not*. We are humans, after all. Very cool side note: did you know Steph Curry of the Golden State Warriors has worked on controlling his heart rate for years? How is he so calm shooting from half court in a buzzer-beater situation? How can he be so chill when an NBA Finals Championship is on the line? An unheard of FOUR championships in a mere eight years when most players have ZERO? He breathes. According to an ESPN Profile by David Flemming [15], Curry can lower his heart rate to 80 simply by controlling his breath and his mind. Incredible. In one 90-second timeout, he can focus on his breath, which lowers his heart rate, and that is what eliminates the anxious jitters and the shaking and creates clarity. Some folks have a resting heart rate up to 100 and they are not playing professional basketball, they are not in the midst of an NBA finals game! So, when you get overly anxious, *breathe deep*.

---

15   Fleming, David. 28 February 2021. *How Stephen Curry's 'organized chaos' fuels his record-breaking career* -- and the Golden State Warriors' rebuild, ESPN, accessed 5 January 2023, https://www.espn.in/nba/story/_/id/30742095/how-stephen-curry-organized-chaos-fuels-record-breaking-career-golden-state-warriors-rebuild

Networking, Outreach, and Interviews

notes

Another tip for these events? Skip the alcohol in excess or all together. It will not make it better or easier. It will dull your mind and make you less sharp. That's going backwards.

Being confident, friendly, and subconsciously a little nervous will put others at ease too. Be a support for them. Not focusing on yourself actually helps. Ask them what they are thinking. Be kind and empathetic. A natural conversation will develop. And by putting in the time to practice your story—not memorizing anything, but knowing that you can rely on yourself—that will help ease your mind. You will know what to say when it's your time to speak. In my glory days of fastpitch softball, my dad used to remind me that practice makes permanent, not perfect. Don't practice to be perfect. Practice to be permanent. Have "story muscle memory" so engrained that you deliver, no matter your nerves. It will become reactive, instinctive. You've got this.

Leveraging LinkedIn for Networking

Today when I present to folks already in the career they want, or already out of teaching, here is the advice I give on building their network and making the network they have stronger:

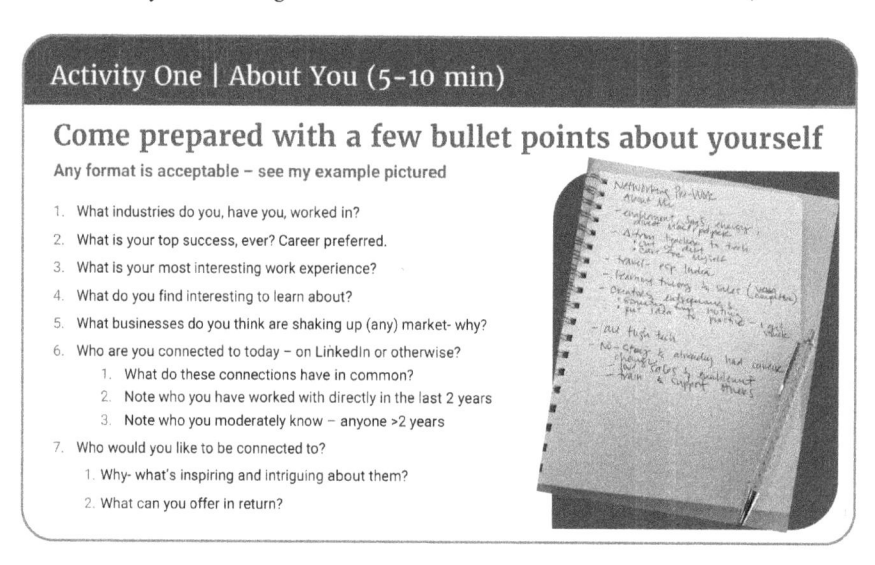

Activity One | About You (5-10 min)

Come prepared with a few bullet points about yourself

Any format is acceptable – see my example pictured

1. What industries do you, have you, worked in?
2. What is your top success, ever? Career preferred.
3. What is your most interesting work experience?
4. What do you find interesting to learn about?
5. What businesses do you think are shaking up (any) market- why?
6. Who are you connected to today – on LinkedIn or otherwise?
   1. What do these connections have in common?
   2. Note who you have worked with directly in the last 2 years
   3. Note who you moderately know – anyone >2 years
7. Who would you like to be connected to?
   1. Why- what's inspiring and intriguing about them?
   2. What can you offer in return?

For you, transitioning out of the classroom, I tweaked it:

- What industries of interest did you research?
- What is your top career success, ever?
  - And how have you related that into business terms?

- Why are you leaving teaching and more importantly, what would you like to be doing?
- What do you find interesting to learn about?
- What businesses (companies, industries, products) are of interest to you?
- Who are you connected to today, on LinkedIn or otherwise?
    - What do these connections have in common?
    - What type of helpful connections are missing (companies, industries, products)?
    - Note who you have worked with directly in the last two years.
    - Note who you moderately know—anyone you've known more than two years.
- Who would you like to be connected to?
    - Why? What's inspiring and intriguing about them?
    - How can they help you?
    - And can you help them in return?

If identifying who you want to reach out to is step one, step two is crafting your outreach.

When on LinkedIn on your laptop, you will click the "connect" button and then click the "add custom note." It is how you start to build the relationship; it shows effort, it can entice the person to accept which is exceptionally helpful if you've never met the person. If you have met the person, you can refer to where and when you met them.

There are a lot of opinions on why this matters. Here's my personal hack. Once the person accepts the connection, the note becomes a LinkedIn message. Those messages are searchable. Super helpful to look up who you met and are now connected with from a conference, and how they discussed a job or shared an idea you want to revisit.

Keep your LinkedIn connection notes short because it's not up to you. LinkedIn puts a 300-character limit on the note, so be succinct. In an email, you can be a bit longer, but no one wants to read a huge email (and they won't), so keep that succinct as well:

- Greeting (make it one word and no need to use their name, that takes up characters)
- How/where you met

Networking, Outreach, and Interviews

notes

- Shared interest or job discussion
- Whatever you said you'd follow up on (like a friendly reminder)

If you have characters left:

- When to contact you back (even if it's a request)

And don't worry about no replies/not-accepted connections. Take it as a sign of fit. It was meant to be, it would be. Move on to the next!

Want to learn more about how to create an impactful LinkedIn profile? Curious to see examples of networking via LinkedIn—the good, the bad, and the ugly? Then check out the online modules that accompany this chapter.

Outreach to Your Network

I remember being 23 years old and living at home at my parent's house in Fenton, MO after graduating from SEMO. I was a bit comfy. I mean I lived there through student teaching the entire semester before. I know now as an adult how lucky I am to have had a family that was in a position to help and support me like they did. My parents have always helped me, which felt a lot different when I was younger.

Everyday my dad would come home from work and ask me, "so how was job hunting?" Like a very good dad, but very annoying to an inexperienced young adult, I heard him say time and time again, "Ashley, you've got to treat looking for a job like it is your job." My little brother can validate this because he too was the recipient of this advice! And so I would. I would do something every day, for hours. Mostly though, I would apply online for EVERY SINGLE SCHOOL DISTRICT. UGH. It was brutal.

Remember 2008? Another down economic time. Every district had their own online portal. Everyone needed the same info. Everyone needed the same uploads—resume, cover letter, references, college transcripts. And in 2008, there was no Google remembering my info for a quick autofill. It wasn't even remembering my credentials! I had written in a notebook every single username and password I had to know. Because OF COURSE some took a unique name, some email, and some required a mess of disparate letters and numbers. I barely got interviews. And when I did, I got passed up. You know why? The jobs went to someone who knew someone. As it turns out, after all that effort, all those hours, all that frustration, I got my job in the fall because I knew someone too.

notes

It was late July. I was desperate. I did not want to go get a job in retail. I put so much pressure on myself. I also couldn't believe that a job was not a slam dunk after college. Going to college was supposed to be the way you got a job; it was a requirement. And yes, the best jobs were competitive. But it wasn't supposed to be that when I graduated there were no jobs. I called my former softball coach who was now an administrator, having left the classroom. I told him I needed help; I had no job. He got me one. It wasn't a classroom teacher role; it was being the study hall monitor. And it paid less than a teacher's salary. You read about this experience already, but that was it. That was my start. After months of applying, it was one phone call that did it.

And then, jump to when I wanted to leave teaching. Still, I wasted so many hours applying online when I should have been networking, meeting people, putting myself and my story out there. My biggest missed opportunity was not making phone calls to people.

- Asking them if I could get five minutes to learn what they did and how they got into it.
- Asking if they knew of an open job and what it was.
- Asking if there was anyone they could introduce me to.
- Asking how I could help. Be involved. Be around.
- Asking if there was something I could be doing for them.

Professional persistence would have served me well. Making calls, following up. If people didn't have helpful information or didn't want to talk, okay. Thank them for their time. On to the next! And not hiding behind email. Even in 2008 it was easier to hide behind a keyboard and send an email than to show up. It can't be that way.

I also acknowledge that not everyone has the same access and connections to make this so easy or get off to an immediate start once you decide to start calling.

How would I go about building my call list?

You did a lot of research as you read this book. We talked a lot about investing time into researching solutions, companies, industries, and jobs you would want. Use the job, industry, company, and solution to do a Google search for a thought leadership or professional development group. Search for related, specific communities. All the information you need to start an informed search is there, so Google those terms in different combinations. Click some links. Refine your

notes

search. Better yet? Click some sponsored returns. I'm serious, and not because I want you to buy what they are selling. Here's why:

Companies spend A LOT of money on marketing—looking to figure out how your mind works and how to get their product in your hands. In designing these strategies, they do much of the thinking for us. They think in advance, "what words are a prospective buyer going to use to search for the solution we sell?" They solve the problem of "how will people search to find us and what words will they look for?"

You will always get paid returns/sponsored (unless your search is unbelievably obscure) and it's awesome if this happens because you may not care about buying anything, BUT most companies are now trying to associate themselves with thought leaders, professional groups, and communities for their customers to share ideas and support one another. Usually on their website there will be some sort of "tie" to this group. Check the company page, client/customer stories page, or the blog page. It makes the search much easier for you.

Once you have the name of an organization you can vet for fit on your own (Google the organization, find their LinkedIn page, see who are members). Some of these groups will be paid membership, but even they have a fair amount of non-member opportunities or information available. I suggest checking out everything that is non-paid first. Officially joining is up to you. If you're unsure, save your money until you are.

Here's a high-level example:

After much thought and refining my findings during my guided exercises from Chapters Three, Five, Six, and Seven:

- I determined that I am competitive, I enjoy a challenge, and I like helping solve problems. I think sales is interesting, I love paid performance, and I like being close to revenue but don't want a quota, and I perform my best work when my goals are clear.
- Having the conversation connecting classroom teaching to corporate training feels the most natural to me (over content development or analyzing data and student performance) and I can visualize myself doing this type of work.
- I care about helping others and I find that I feel when I coach them to succeed, I too succeed.
- From there, sales enablement and sales training stood out as jobs I could do that would combine my strong teaching and presentation skills combined with the challenge of training those on skills necessary to close a sale and knowing

notes

who I was training had a high expectation of me and that company revenue could be better or worse depending on how good I was. In staying in training and coaching I could help solve problems of my trainees and make them better.
- I googled "sales training revenue enablement community thought leadership."

My first 10 non-sponsored returns were gold mines!

- There were multiple paid and unpaid organizations to join! (I can find these organizations on LinkedIn and get names of members to connect with.)
- There was a podcast about sales enablement.
- There was a published marketing report about the profession.
- There was a related field to learn more about (RevOps or Revenue Operations) (good for interviews and knowing how to work with other departments. The ability to make change and connect internally matters.).
- There were some companies that returned that did not pay to be there. They returned because the match of their content to my search was a great fit.

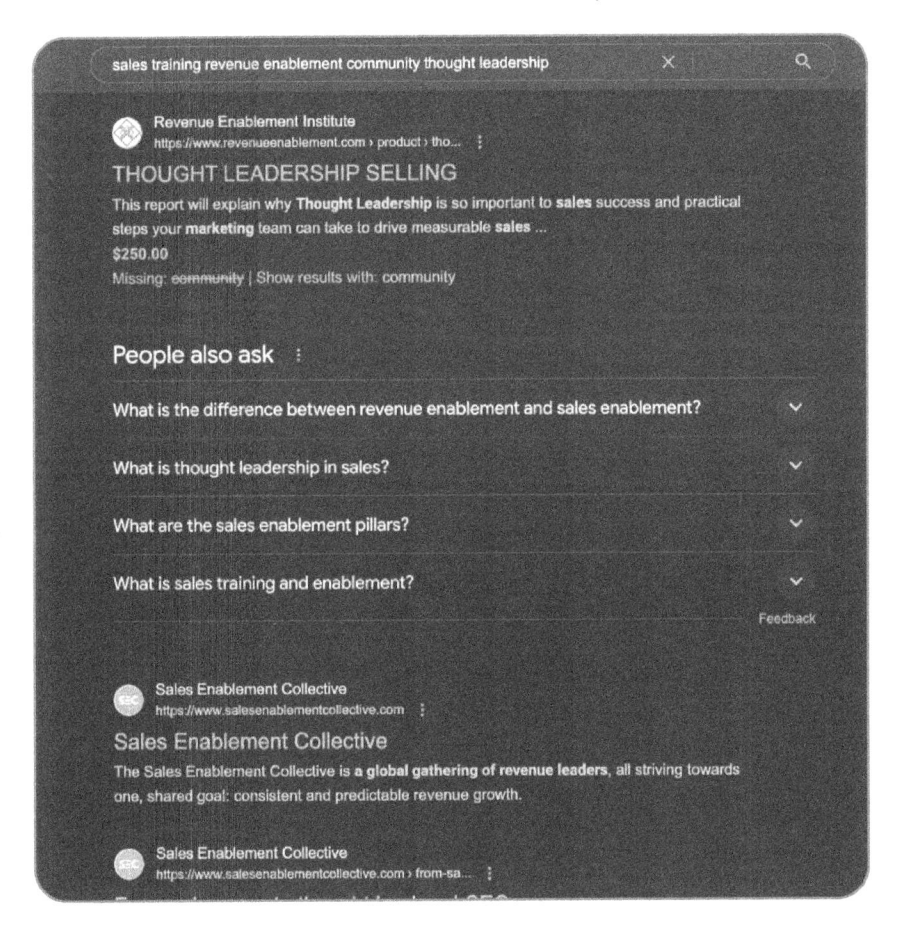

Networking, Outreach, and Interviews

177

notes

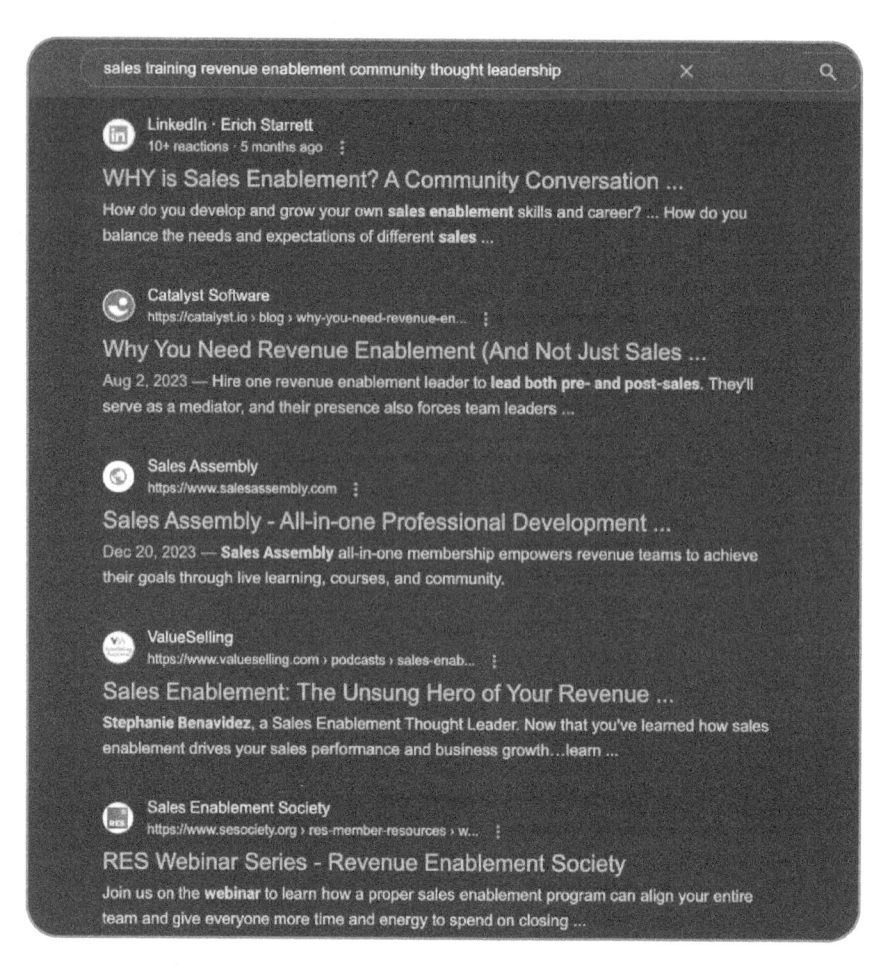

---

sales training revenue enablement community thought leadership

LinkedIn · Erich Starrett
10+ reactions · 5 months ago

WHY is Sales Enablement? A Community Conversation ...
How do you develop and grow your own **sales enablement** skills and career? ... How do you balance the needs and expectations of different **sales** ...

Catalyst Software
https://catalyst.io › blog › why-you-need-revenue-en...

Why You Need Revenue Enablement (And Not Just Sales ...
Aug 2, 2023 — Hire one revenue enablement leader to **lead both pre- and post-sales**. They'll serve as a mediator, and their presence also forces team leaders ...

Sales Assembly
https://www.salesassembly.com

Sales Assembly - All-in-one Professional Development ...
Dec 20, 2023 — **Sales Assembly** all-in-one membership empowers revenue teams to achieve their goals through live learning, courses, and community.

ValueSelling
https://www.valueselling.com › podcasts › sales-enab...

Sales Enablement: The Unsung Hero of Your Revenue ...
Stephanie Benavidez, a Sales Enablement Thought Leader. Now that you've learned how sales enablement drives your sales performance and business growth…learn ...

Sales Enablement Society
https://www.sesociety.org › res-member-resources › w...

RES Webinar Series - Revenue Enablement Society
Join us on the **webinar** to learn how a proper sales enablement program can align your entire team and give everyone more time and energy to spend on closing ...

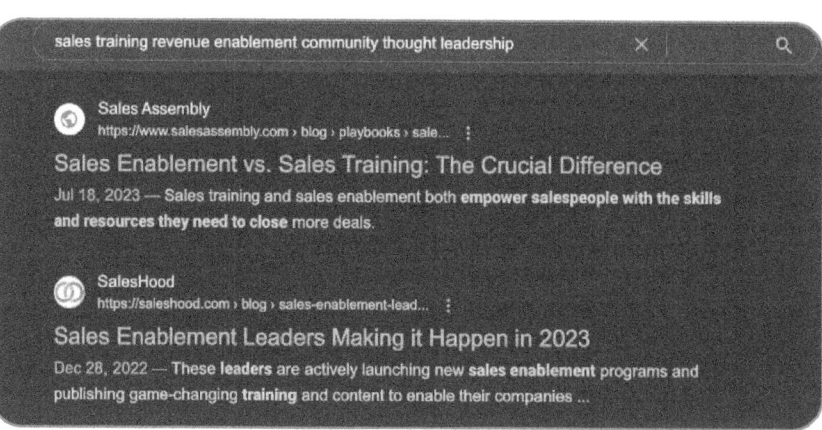

---

sales training revenue enablement community thought leadership

Sales Assembly
https://www.salesassembly.com › blog › playbooks › sale...

Sales Enablement vs. Sales Training: The Crucial Difference
Jul 18, 2023 — Sales training and sales enablement both **empower salespeople with the skills and resources they need to close** more deals.

SalesHood
https://saleshood.com › blog › sales-enablement-lead...

Sales Enablement Leaders Making it Happen in 2023
Dec 28, 2022 — These **leaders** are actively launching new **sales enablement** programs and publishing game-changing **training** and content to enable their companies ...

notes

My top four sponsored (meaning a company paid to be there) returns were just as helpful!

- All would have given me more companies to potentially make connections at.
- I learned more about the market and checked if they had open roles.
- I could find the names of communities to network in, including attending in-person events and conferences.

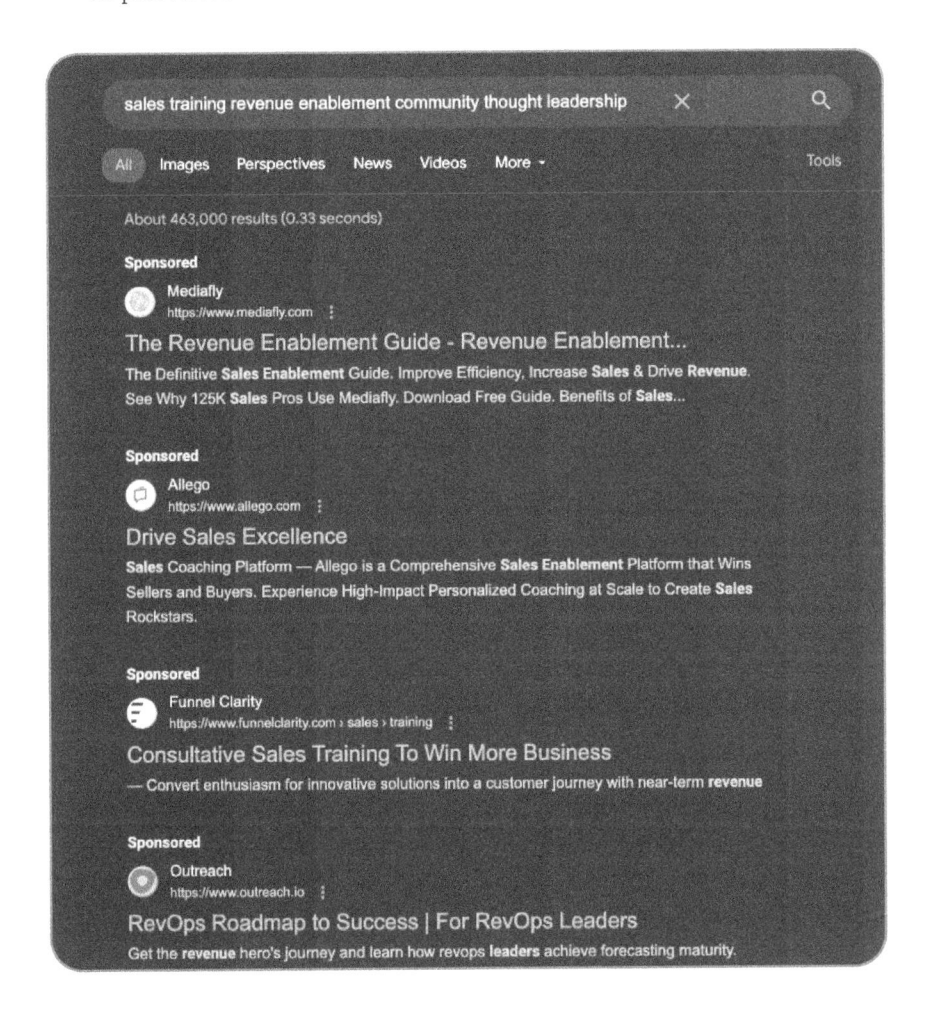

![Screenshot of Google search results for "sales training revenue enablement community thought leadership" showing About 463,000 results (0.33 seconds). Four sponsored results are displayed: Mediafly — "The Revenue Enablement Guide - Revenue Enablement..."; Allego — "Drive Sales Excellence"; Funnel Clarity — "Consultative Sales Training To Win More Business"; Outreach — "RevOps Roadmap to Success | For RevOps Leaders".]

Networking, Outreach, and Interviews

notes

This is something you can easily do for yourself.

If you really want to make an impact for yourself, take your search returns a few steps further:

1. Call the organizations you find. Talk to them. There is a phone number on the website.
    a. Is there a local chapter?
    b. Are there in-person events? Virtual?
    c. Do they have an open-access job board?
    d. How can people connect?
2. Connect with the suggested people from #1.
3. Go to the events. Make the right connections.
    a. Ask how they got into the industry/career.
    b. Ask if they know of an open job and what is it, where is it?
    c. Ask if there is anyone they could introduce you to.
    d. Ask how you can help. Be involved. Be around.
    e. Ask what they need. What support are they seeking?
4. Attend free, open webinars from the same organizations or companies.
    a. Connect with other attendees.

These types of in-person connections become your call network for the next role; the role that includes a raise, a better fit, and more opportunity.

Outreach to Recruiters and Hiring Managers

Reaching out to recruiters and hiring managers is a bit different than networking for peers or industry/role connections. With your LinkedIn DMs and email follow-ups from virtual or in-person networking events, you can be more informal. There usually isn't a clear goal other than to mutually agree upon helping each other, when/if the time comes. You build on those connections to stay current in industry topics and learning opportunities.

When a job is on the line, the possibility of an interview, the outreach is different. It is formal, it is succinct, and it needs to show a connection between YOU and the JOB/COMPANY. With a recruiter or hiring manager, you most likely have not met them. In business this is considered "cold" outreach (you're right in suspecting that if you've met briefly or are introduced, that would be "warm").

We all prefer warm—this is why you call around and ask if there is someone you can be introduced to. But again, I understand as you build a network, you're more likely to rely on cold outreach, especially when you're first starting out.

Here are the tips I share. I can't say this will have an amazing success rate. It's like a half step up from applying online; however, you will never know if you don't try.

When you reach out to a recruiter or hiring manager,

- Keep it succinct; too long and it won't get read (they get hundreds of notes when a job is available, plus thousands of applicants).
- You can skip the long intro ("My name is…and I'm inquiring about…").
- In your intro (one sentence, maybe two if it's a really good sentence), explain why you want to be at that company.
  - What stood out to you in your research?
  - What did you find that makes it a great culture fit for you?
  - Where is the company successful today and how can you keep that momentum going, add to it, make it better?
- Tie your top one or two skills to the job description.
  - Don't pick tactical elements (like designing a training [lesson]).
  - Pick something big (designing the entire strategy for alignment [like curriculum]).
  - Talk about making your customers happy. Who are your customers? The job description tells you.
    - » You made parents and students happy and engaged, smoothed over negative feelings—you can do this again with their clients, internal employees, etc.
- Share a success story that maps to what the job description says needs solving.
  - Ex: the job description says you will train junior sales reps to sell the new product.
  - Tell a story about how you took a brand-new state standard and got x% of your students competent/passed.
- Don't worry about being 'overly formal.' It's okay to be yourself. You don't want to speak in slang or shorthand, like a text, but no need to refer to a thesaurus.

notes

- But do mind your spelling, big grammar no-nos (like run-on sentences), and typos. For me? I love commas. I use them incorrectly all the time. That does not stop me from sending emails. 🙂

Interview Tips and Preparation

I've felt that my interviews often include my hiring manager telling me they were told about me already (good things) but a bit annoyed (or maybe that was my anxiety, perhaps curious is what they were) of who could I possibly be that I suddenly am inserted into the situation? It was a good question from them, I loved it. Everyone wants a warm intro!

Then they all asked me, "what could I do?" That question didn't shake me for long. I learned by doing my first few jobs how many transferable skills I had. I was sure that I knew what I could do and why I'd be good at it. I had talking points ready if I needed to use them.

And the times I went in cold from a recruiter setting up the appointment, I went in confident. Really shaky inside and definitely sweating, but again, gotta breathe, smile, and get through it. I'll keep saying it: confidence goes a long way.

I also went into the interview wanting to ensure the other person understood I was a great teammate. That I was an excellent follower and leader. That those could be interchangeable and congruent as the situation required.

I also was sure to ask about them, who they were, at the start of the interview. I didn't want to have to wait until the end of the interview to make this interaction feel more like a conversation. Many times, people think that if they are being interviewed, they are silent until asked to speak and the topic to speak on is provided. My gosh, it's not an interrogation.

It's a conversation. Treat it as such.

When they ask me how I am, I answer and then I ask back.

When they say, "tell me about yourself," I do and then I ask them back.

When they ask about my career history, I say that I used to be a teacher; I always make a point to start there. I tell it every time. It's an exceptionally short, drama-free rendition. But I don't hide it. Then I get into my tech/enablement career.

They always have a comment about teaching. I can always squeeze in one more personal question to build the relationship before the rest of the interview is more traditional Q&A. My teaching past has always gotten me a follow-up question or a shared curiosity and it's been a way that I can articulate more about myself. And what did I share? Duh! Something about me that related to the job I was there for! I didn't talk about something random, I prepared.

Interviews are all about presenting why YOU are the right person to help fill their gap, solve their problem, or address their need. The more you can tailor your answers to articulate that, being as specific as you can, the more you will stand out and have the hiring manager needing you for their team.

How would I go about preparing for interviews? I'm about to sound like a broken record here. Have I mentioned research? Do it.

Before you go into the interview, do these things:

- Once you have an interview or phone screening set, look up who you will be meeting with (look up the company leadership on the website). Find commonalities where you can—interests, skills, volunteer work, past jobs, college attended, interests.
    - Get this name by asking the person who set it up.
    - Get it from the meeting invite or emails.
- Look up who you think your possible teammates will be (LinkedIn). Find commonalities where you can. In LinkedIn:
    - Go to the company page.
    - Click on "people."
    - Search by department name (get from the job description) or ask the recruiter what department you'd be part of.
    - Get bold and connect with a few—but you MUST add a custom note. Tell them you are interviewing and ask what they like about the company and the team. If they reply, this may be good info to bring up in the interview. Plus, you may hit it off and then they might send a positive note to the manager. Why not?
- Research who are customers and why they are happy.
    - Go to the case studies or related tab on the website.
    - Look for posts on the company LinkedIn page.
    - Watch client testimonials on the website or YouTube.
- Watch the marketing and product materials on YouTube.
- Look up the leadership team (again, big signal on culture—is there diversity???).

Networking, Outreach, and Interviews

notes

- Prepare questions you have as you research.
  - Ask about the team, who they are, their tenure (this can be where you talk about who you already connected with and the positive from that).
  - Tell what you found and ask what the current initiatives are.
- Find recent press releases (for real, companies make them all the time).

> And a MUST, MUST is to look at any materials the company gives you.

If you don't look and they ask a question, they will know you're faking it, most likely. If you haven't even peeked? That's a problem. But I know you'd never do that—because you are putting in so much work right now to get that opportunity. I know you'll make the most of it!

Whatever materials they give you, they might also give instructions. If they do, prepare the best you can: a presentation, a method or approach you'd take to solve the problem, a specific story of how you did this job before (or closely related). If there are no instructions, they might just ask for a general reaction. You'll be ready because you did the checklist above in preparation. Lean on what you learned, what stood out, and why you're the best fit.

As "rounds" of interviews go by and you make it through, repeat the list above for the next audience. This will get easier because you'll have the basics down.

As the interviews go deeper, you'll want to get more refined in your questions and continue to map stories to the job. And it's okay to tell the same success story to another person. If you're worried about it, before you get into telling your story (answer to their question), simply ask, "I told this to the Name of First Interviewer, did they share it with you?" If they say no, then tell it. If they say yes, ask if they have questions about it, or tell it again with different or deeper details, or ask if they'd like to hear a different story. Whatever they say, do that.

Don't dread the end or be surprised when the interview ends with "do you have any questions?" This is unbelievably standard. Have 1-3 questions prepared. Here is my list:

1. I ALWAYS ask about company culture, and I ask it this way:
   a. What excites you the most about working at ABC company and leading this team? I'm listening for teamwork, paid volunteer days, time off, balance, leadership opportunities, groups to get involved in, etc.

2. I ask a clarifying question about the job itself. Job descriptions are impossibly long most of the time. If you read it, you'll have at least one question. If not, fake it and ask anyway. Show you took the time to read it.

    a. A tip? Bring a pen and paper and jot down notes or words to trigger your brain to come back to a topic. It will show you were listening and engaged, and it will be a relevant follow-up question.

3. Ask any question that clarifies the next step. Even if you don't ask it as a question, but rather say, "last thing is, I want to confirm the next step is XYZ. Yes?" It shows you care and that you will be ready.

Here's a tip on asking questions at the end. Refrain from asking questions like,

- So, do you think I'm a good fit?
- What gives you pause about me in this role?
- Do you think the team will like me? That I will fit in?

These types of questions show a lack of confidence, for the most part. You may be concerned about these things, but you don't want to come off as insecure. If you do want to know more and are curious if you are a fit, then ask something like, "tell me more about the team members and how they work together and collaborate." If you love the answer, say, "me too! I do my best work when I XYZ." If you don't like the answer, be polite and you'll want to keep searching for a place you will like.

Last bit of advice, especially in later stages: think outside the box (recall my story about the new product feature and selling against the competition). Find a way to stand out and make connections with the people you meet. People want to work with people they can get along with and know can complete the work. Show you can be that great teammate.

You'll want to be sure to keep constant and professional communication through the process. Talk to the recruiter on the phone? Email them thank you and a few sentences to confirm the next steps and what you discussed. Interview? Absolutely send a thank you email (grab their email from the meeting invite. At least find them on LinkedIn and send it that way).

Not the news you wanted and told they went with another candidate? Still send a thank you; say that you appreciate the opportunity, say what you enjoyed about the conversation and the company, and ask them to keep you in mind for future roles now that they know more about you.

Sticking With It

In the next chapter, you'll hear about others' successful transitions from teaching, but one teaser:

> Almost everyone wanted to share how much opportunity continues to come their way in their new careers.

The skills you've gained in the classroom, your certifications, and your degrees? The work you did in these exercises to refine and make them work for you in a new role and a new career is not easy. It is not an average amount of work. You're doing this while you have a full-time job. I cannot stress how much I hope YOU can see yourself in a new career as much as I can. It is possible. Teachers are amazing professionals who are more skilled than your average bear.

Yet, I stop hearing from folks all the time. Teachers who reached out and were So ReAdY tO LeAVe. Emotional, exhausted, broke...and they disappear. It's more common than I'm comfortable with. Not that I take it personally in any way. I'm uncomfortable because I know the person decided to stay. To stay, to wake up every day and feel the same way. Breaks my heart.

I have thought about why this happens. I think it's that the fear coupled with the amount of effort needed (required) to make a quality change seems (is, becomes) overwhelming. To put it into perspective, most teachers earn a four-year degree, spend years learning and practicing teaching in a semi-controlled environment, and study and pass exams all to prepare for this career we call classroom teaching.

Now you're trying to insert yourself into the workforce at an accelerated pace, skipping the formal training this time, and there is a lot to learn. Teachers don't realize that in business, you hear "no" a heck of a lot more times than "yes." But you don't need a yes every time, just one time.

So, I'm always delighted when I get a note like this one:

> Hello Ashley!
> Thanks for checking in on me. I apologize for taking such a long time to reply. I have been kind of in a holding pattern. I've really been on the fence about leaving. I think it's just hard to take those first steps, put yourself out there, and, likely, fail. I am not so practiced in the art of failing gracefully with regards to my work. I also just want to make sure a move to a new career is what is best for my family.
> However, last night, by some divine providence, I ran into someone I had not seen for 7 years at our sons' basketball game. She used to work for ____, worked for ____ and now sells for ____ in their higher ed department. She and I talked and she said the SAME things you did. I have added her on LinkedIn and she is going to work to help get me connected to some people as well. I am finalizing my CV today and am going to fumble my way forward...
> I am SO nervous to start connecting with strangers that don't know me from Adam and try to promote myself with humility (which may be my theme of 2024)!
> Christie

Your courage is admirable. It is okay if you start and stop. If it takes longer than you'd like. You now have incredible networking skills to keep building. Or maybe you'll get it right the first time. Let me be the first to congratulate Future You!

You will have more balance in your life. More time to give to personal and professional pursuits.

In my post-teacher career, I feel like I've yet to hit my ceiling. I love being a lifelong learner. I read one to two books on a general business topic a month and as a result, not only have I grown in skill and role, but promotion. Most often I'm reading about a method, a study, a story, a new way. These are some of my favorite topics:

- Customer success
- Marketing plans and social media
- Women in leadership roles
- GTM strategy and (my favorite!!) the next phase of...
- ...Tactical plan design and change management
- Investing and personal finances
- Skills: Prioritizing, planning, resilience, negotiation
- Lean design—in manufacturing and company design

It is because I changed my career that I have time to continue to invest in myself. When I was a teacher, I was exhausted. I could barely read a fiction book every other month, much less upskill myself reading non-fiction on top of that.

When you get that first non-classroom teacher job, whether you decide to keep climbing or take in the current view, enjoy all the hard-earned perks of investing in yourself and overcoming the stigma.

Now What?

These activities will be time-consuming. I would not rush through it. You get one "at bat" with these folks. On the flip side, nothing changes if nothing changes. So, waiting a good bit of time and talking yourself out of picking up the phone or clicking send won't help either.

To make you more comfortable, I've prioritized your outreach in five steps, putting lowest risk first.

ONE:

Flip your "open to" radio button in LinkedIn and choose if you want the banner or not. Be sure your headline includes the new job title and jargon about that role so your name comes up in search results.

TWO:

Identify who your network is today. It may be small, and that's ok. Who is in it?

- Acquaintances
- Friends of friends or friends of family members
- College connections or certification program connections
- Other teachers who left—either to a new career or moved on from your campus and won't hint to your current principal/campus

THREE:

Do a Google search as I described earlier in the chapter to build your list of potential connections. In addition to individuals, be sure to include related thought leadership experts as well as professional groups. Check out any vendors or service providers who return in your search. You can follow these companies on LinkedIn, too.

FOUR:

Refer to the list of questions you built in Chapter Six of what you'd ask someone already in the role you desire to be in.

Using a LinkedIn search, find people in the role and send your customized connection request asking if they would meet with you for 15 minutes. When you do set up time, ask your planned questions and take notes. Don't forget to ask them who they network with and what groups they follow and learn from.

Don't talk yourself out of this important conversation. Imagine another teacher asked you to meet with them on how you run your classroom procedures because they wanted to learn more. You'd say sure. I bet you'll get this vibe too from people in the entry/early-level roles.

FIVE:

Let's plan your outreach. For each person, bullet out what you'd say, more of a brain dump. Then refine your list to the most important 1-3 things to ask. One item should always be who is hiring and can you be introduced.

Thought leaders:

To start, follow them only, for now.

Reach out once you digest their content and have a more robust understanding of their viewpoint of the market and the role. These folks interact with thousands of people. A connection would be great! But simply learning from them will help up your business acumen so you can talk the talk in your direct outreach to others.

Then once you find a role you really want, reach out and ask if they know anyone at that company and if they would be willing to introduce you.

For individuals you know today:

Calling them is best. Practice with a friend, role play, then make the call.

- Ask them if they know of any opportunities in the area you want to be in.
- Ask if they can connect you with anyone else who might know of opportunities.
- Thank them for their time and ask them to keep you in mind should they hear of anything.

Professional groups:

If there is a phone number, call and ask for more information. If an email, send your questions there. Follow up as much as you can in joining, searching a job board (if they have one), and attending free events—both in person and virtual.

Remember, if it's paid and you're unsure, it is okay to wait and learn more if it's the right fit for you before parting with your hard-earned money.

For individuals you don't know:

Email them if you can find an address; otherwise, a LinkedIn message is fine (just keep in mind the 300-character limitation).

- Write that you're interested in making a career change to your desired role.
- Do they know of anyone hiring?
- Is there an individual or a group they could introduce you to?
- Thank them.

Once engaged in a back-and-forth conversation, don't forget to keep in mind to offer any way you can help them as well. There might not be anything immediately, but it's important to show reciprocity.

Recruiters:

Search on LinkedIn to find ones in your industry or associated with jobs you want. Craft your notes to them.

1. Explain why you're interested in this new career.
2. Tell a related success.
3. Explain why you're a great fit—both skills and culture.

You'll only reach out to a hiring manager and potential teammates once you find a specific job and use the People search on the company page to identify them.

10

Success!
Interviews and Advice From Teachers Who Made a Career Change
(and LOVE it!)

I know I wrote "trust me" a few times in this book. I didn't do a keyword search to find out the exact number of times. However, I do know that trust is earned and built over time. It is a privilege to earn someone's trust. Since we haven't known each other that long, what I can provide to get your buy-in on my approach is to share the stories of other people who have successfully exited the classroom.

These are all people I know, in full transparency. I talk to them. I stayed true to the messages and advice they wanted to share. So maybe you don't exactly trust me implicitly, but perhaps hearing these shared experiences and similar advice from others will give you the courage to trust in the process and change your life.

It can be done!

notes

Meet my friend, Christian.

He's a former high school geometry teacher.
Today he's a senior actuarial analyst.

I talked about Christian in the book before now. He is the most country Long Islander I know, thanks to our time teaching together in Texas. We have quite a few other similarities in our past relationships, but that's not why I consider him a friend. He's my friend because of who he is. He loves his family, he is true to himself, and the man can barbecue like no other. Not kidding, he made some of the best hot wings I've ever had one day after school when he hosted a happy hour for a group of us. I'm proud of Christian. He has built a life he loves.

When did you know you wanted a change?

During the first year I kept telling myself *next year will be better*. A month into year two, I realized *there was no way I could do this again*.

It wasn't anything specific, more of a nagging feeling. I realized I wasn't a strong teacher when it came to skills and I became miserable. There were a lot of behavior issues on campus (gangs, racial tensions); at times it felt like more issues than the administration team could handle. Most kids were not engaged and I found myself, right or wrong, giving them a pass and focusing on students who cared, investing in the students who wanted help.

What steps did you take to leave?

I started with the question—what else can I do with a mathematics degree?

- I Googled my question and "teacher, actuary, and research assistant" returned.
- I looked into options and thought actuary seemed realistic. I focused my efforts there.
- I began studying for exams while still in the classroom.
- I told myself, I'm going all in and seeing where this goes.

What have been your most transferable skills from classroom to corporate?

- Openness to learning new ways, to new ideas, to new processes.
- Listen to feedback and then make changes so I can improve.

notes

What would you do differently?

I should have listened to my gut during student teaching. I knew I was screwed and this was not the profession for me. I wish I would have paused teaching, chosen a new major and spent two more years in college. Not ideal, but it would not have been the end of the world.

What advice would you give to someone also looking to make this change?

Ultimately, when you leave campus at the end of the day exhausted and already dreading tomorrow? That sucks and is not a good quality of life. Working sucks, but you have to do it, so make it as least sucky as possible! Find something enjoyable to do with your life rather than sit in misery.

Don't tell yourself you can't because there is someone out there willing to take a chance on you.

Just do it.

Meet my friend, Penny.

She's a former high school physical science, physics, and chemistry teacher.
Today she's a vice president of global learning.

I met Penny because we are both customers of the same software we use to train, coach, and support our respective sales teams. We've attended several of the same conferences and recently spoke at the same event. Penny is impressive when it comes to her craft; I always learn from her. I don't recall how, but it didn't take long for us to realize we were both teachers in our past careers. Penny is a wonderful person with a heart of service. Meeting and connecting with people like Penny are why it's worth it to go to networking events. You'll read about Penny again as she has been a great support in helping other teachers transition into a new career.

What was the catalyst for you to leave teaching?

I realized during the first semester of year nine it felt like I was living Groundhog Day. It's not like any new elements popped up on the periodic table and I couldn't stomach the repetition of *teaching it again*.

Coupled with around year four or five I was Teacher of the Year, a finalist in the state running, and the school just kept piling on more and more stressors. Eventually I had a majority of the IEPs, the 504s, the largest class sizes. *It felt like, really??*

notes

This was at the same time unions got heavily involved in contracts and there was heavy negotiation pressure and *I found myself becoming the crabby teacher I never wanted to be.*

What steps did you take to leave?

My journey is a bit different. I worked in a chemistry laboratory in product development as a first career, then went into teaching. When I decided to leave the classroom, I looked to get back into being a chemist, but after being gone for almost 10 years, I was no longer qualified as my skills were outdated.

I decided to look up jobs in sales.

What do you do now? What's been your career path since the classroom?

Today I'm in charge of training the sales team, client success team, and channel partners at a software company. I work with sales and revenue leaders to determine what is needed to impact revenue. I then design and implement the necessary training, polishing of skills, and methods to increase customer satisfaction.

What have been your most transferable skills from classroom to corporate?

- Presentation skills—and we [teachers] can pull one out of anywhere!
- Project management.
- Customer service—in teaching I supported 150 student, parent, and principal clients daily and kept them on track. I asked one hiring manager early on, *do you service 150 clients a day?* She did not!
- Working with a variety of people, personalities, quirks, and learning styles.

What advice would you give to someone also looking to make this change?

Don't waste your time on resumes and online applications. Call everyone you know and ask if they know of any open jobs, who is hiring, and would this person vouch for you and introduce you to anyone else who might be able to help you. Calling and networking is key.

Ignore the self-doubt. You are harder on yourself than others will be because you are not *just a teacher*. Be bold: you have the necessary skills, you just need to learn to describe them in business language.

Meet my friend, Danica.

She's a former first grade and kindergarten teacher.
Today she's a customer success manager.

I met Danica because I knew Penny. I received a DM one day asking if I would be open to meeting Danica, an exhausted and done-with-the-classroom teacher. I would have said "yes" no matter what, but coming from Penny, not only did I want to help, I was determined to give it my best.

Danica already had a great start putting to work the advice and tips Penny shared. I was able to support her in determining her transferable classroom skills for interview prep, role playing, tweaking her presentation, and stories. Because Danica is a talented professional who happens to have been a teacher first, she landed a wonderful job and began a new career.

When did you know you wanted a change?

When I finally realized enough was enough. I was sitting in my car outside of the school during the second week in October. I called my dad and I told him I wanted to stop teaching. That was the moment I decided I needed to make a change. He told me he had been waiting for me to say something. He knew I was unhappy, but I had to realize it for myself.

Why did you want to change your career and leave teaching?

There are many reasons why. College was simply not enough preparation for the classroom. Each year I had a new grade, which meant a new curriculum to learn. Then in my fourth year, three days after the start of the school year, they made me move my entire classroom and changed the grade I taught. They made this change at the end of the day on Wednesday and told me I had to be ready to teach the next Monday. Also, COVID was really hard to navigate and they were constantly changing how we graded/assessed our kids.

Ultimately, I wanted to leave because teaching no longer served me. It took me time to reconcile the feelings I had around leaving. However, that day in the car I thought to myself, *"Why stay? Really, why?"* There were too many reasons to leave and not nearly enough reasons to stay. So, I left.

What immediate steps did you take to make a change? What worked? What didn't?

The hardest part in leaving was truly not knowing what to do. I Googled "teacher leave teaching" and "transition jobs." I didn't have a LinkedIn and I didn't know how to find other teachers like me—ones that wanted to leave and had successfully left.

What worked was networking. It really is all about who you know and who you can meet. I called friends and connections of my parents and family friends. This was true for teaching—I got my job because someone I knew working in the district went to the principal on my behalf. While networking for a new career, I found people willing to help me with my resume, interview support, and role plays. Ashley and my brother helped by practicing with me and providing feedback.

What didn't work was using Indeed. It got me nowhere and I wasted so much time and effort.

Listening to podcasts and stories was informative but didn't lead to jobs.

What have been your most transferable skills from classroom to corporate?

- Creating learning materials and training content for my customers.
- Building out exercises [activities] for their training programs.
- Curriculum development and content best practices.
- Understanding time management and strong organization skills.
- Communication.
- Understanding what's important to the learner or audience and speaking to that.

What advice would you give to someone also looking to make this change?

I wish I had known from the start that I had more to offer. I learned the hard way. *I let my lack of confidence slow me down and get in the way of growth.* Had I realized I was better than I understood, *I could have focused on being a sponge versus being worried I wasn't good enough.*

So many of my teacher colleagues were unhappy but they chose to stay stuck in misery. There are so many people who need to be encouraged to leave any job, any industry, if you are unhappy. *I want to scream that life is too short to sit in a job you hate.*

notes

Meet my friend, Crystal.

She's a former multi-grade elementary and middle school teacher in public and private schools.
Today she's a solution specialist (architect), Director of Enterprise Accounts.

I met Crystal through a referral from a co-worker for an open role I was hiring for. I trusted this person and didn't think twice about them making a referral. Crystal was looking to leave the classroom and get into a new career where she could also build upon her strengths earned while running a side business. Not surprising, I 100% give teachers a shot in the interview process as I believe they are highly skilled.

Crystal put in more effort to get her role than any of the other candidates combined. She was enthusiastic, and boy could I tell she put in the time and effort to research the company. In her interview she put together an awesome demo of a software of her choice. She nailed it. It was tailored to the role she wanted, presented how our clients wanted to see information, and her grasp of business jargon (knowing it was the company's job to train her) was admirable. She got the job and has excelled since day one. She is a trusted resource not only for the sales team she supports, but for many departments within the company.

How did you know it was time to pursue a new career?

I left teaching second grade at a public school to take a job at a private school teaching fifth and sixth grade since my family was moving. This was supposed to be a better move though, a private school. But right away I didn't like the school or the grades I was assigned. It was glorified public school except the administration let the parents walk all over the teachers because these were the wealthy families of a rural area. It was an environment that let a few folks with a little bit of money treat teachers like "the help."

Then COVID came. It was during the height of it that I realized I wasn't just unhappy, I hated the job.

What immediate steps did you take to make a change? What worked? What didn't?

I began talking to people. I would ask them questions like: what job they did, did they like it, what was the comp/pay range of the job, and if their company was hiring.

Next I put together a resume but I chose someone who wasn't really in tune with how to help a teacher translate their skills, nor were they familiar with technology-

notes

focused roles, so that wasn't as helpful as it could have been. I also spent quite a bit of time looking at software that job postings said I had to be "proficient" in. But none of the jobs really required that much and once I got a job I was given the training I needed (this is more like advice, but don't spend too much time learning everything, just get familiar).

What did work was at a Friendsgiving I was talking to an acquaintance and asked the typical questions. She told me about an open solution architect role, what I would be doing, and that there were a few experienced team members I could learn a lot from. She said she would refer me and that I should apply so that she could let the company know.

What have been your most transferable skills from classroom to corporate?

The skill I'd share as the most useful is using data to make decisions. Data sounds scary, but it's not. You just have to know what you are looking at. Usually in my job it's simple things and not overly complex.

I'd compare what I do today to looking at MAP scores (reading or math). We'd test the students 2x a year (early in the year and late) and the change in scores helped us place the students in the right reading group and determine what book(s) they were ready for and if we should push them. For clients, I look at the data we have and use it to answer "will this be effective for the client and what the market can handle?" and "should I offer this to clients based on the volumes they are doing?"

Other transferable skills:

- Flexibility—the constant changing and adjusting to the client needs is so similar to the classroom that was also constantly changing and meeting student needs.
- Adjust and adapt to your audience—meet the student where they are; now it's meeting a colleague or client where they are when I'm relaying information.
- Presentation skills and engagement—capturing the audience and being able to change. I demo the same platform just like the content doesn't change. What changes is how I present it for my client, like I did for my kids. For example, the same program for reading, I'd meet the kids where they are at: how I say it, show it, discuss it. And if the student (or client!) doesn't understand or doesn't care, I have to adapt to that.
- Keeping receipts—the importance of documentation! Noting what is happening in the company and what the client needs is very similar to documenting student needs and progress.

What advice would you give to someone also looking to make this change?

Once you determine the industry you want to be in, ask a lot of questions when you find someone in the industry. Ask about clients, what they care about, what a day in the life of the job looks like.

- To connect with people so you can start asking more questions, relate to them. Look them up on their website or LinkedIn and what they tell you they care about, weave that into the conversation. (Ex: I saw a person I wanted to connect with was a volunteer at The United Way event and I wove that into the conversation. It was very helpful!)
- Sign up for blogs and newsletters for the industry and then ask people in the industry to explain it to you. People will help.
- Find out who they know in the company. Can they help you get your foot in the door and get you a convo and an interview? This is the biggest thing, and make sure the person you are asking is a reputable person.

Get a resume writer to help you. Make sure they are skilled at resume writing for the roles and industry you want to work in.

Leaving teaching can be scary because it becomes your identity and we tell ourselves and are told by others we are "just teachers." Now, when I'm asked my opinion, it's because I'm respected and have input. As a teacher it was lip service, and my voice didn't have weight. Now I have autonomy.

Meet my friend, Anthony.

He's a former first and second grade and middle school teacher.
Today he's a senior sales director.

I had the pleasure of meeting Anthony while I was running onboarding and leading "sales bootcamps." He was a new sales rep at the company I worked for. At the time, onboarding was delivered via a software platform I managed, but was coupled with a week of intensive in-person training (the "bootcamp"). The company was a bit chaotic, as I've already written, and Anthony was someone who kept me sane. He experienced just as much crazy as I did. Even through the chaos, it was easy to see that Anthony was someone who cared about his clients, worked hard to create connections and build relationships, and strived to do the right thing.

Even today Anthony's story of resilience, commitment to helping others, and doing the right thing gives me tingles. His experience in the classroom was a rough one, and like me, leaving was just as turbulent. Today, Anthony is settled, successful, and most importantly, happy.

How did you know it was time to pursue a new career?

It was my third year of teaching in inner-city Philadelphia. Three different campuses, three different grades. The difficulties of the community carried right on into the schools, it was a very difficult environment. I was often pushed, hit, cursed out, and saw a lot of violence. A veteran teacher of ~20 years was my mentor. Unfortunately there was an incident with a student in his classroom where the student was blatantly insubordinate and it got very physical between them. I watched this good teacher snap. He broke. *All I could think was, if I stayed that would be me too. That was not the future I wanted. It was not why I got into teaching.*

What was your path out of the classroom?

I had been in marketing before teaching and I left because I decided I wanted to give more, to help. I wanted summer off to write for enjoyment. For me, that meant teaching. While I was in the classroom, I earned a master's degree. But when I decided to leave the classroom, I started bartending to make ends meet and honestly, *I needed a comedown from teaching.*

I ended up calling a contact who led a business development team and I became a BDR for the sales team. I did really well; I was often the top performer on the team. Eventually I took on a role training other sales roles at the company. One of the training programs I led was focused on leadership development and upskilling. This training job allowed me to blend my talents: my education, my teaching skills, and the desire to help others. I also got the opportunity to speak at conferences due to my success and was a requested trainer by employees. Over time the culture changed and it was no longer a fit. I got back into sales and this time took on an elevated role as quota carrier in EdTech EdTech.

What have been your most transferable skills from classroom to corporate?

If you choose to get into EdTech or education companies, you have so much pedagogy. You understand curriculum and lesson design, you get LMS, and you know how to train people.

Keep in mind, hard [job/role specific] skills, the company will teach you. *Teachers have incredible soft skills*; we can see what is going to happen and get in front of it:

- Communication, breaking down topics.
- Understanding your audience and the mindset of who you are talking to.
- Situational awareness and amazing peripheral vision.

- Data analysis of students is useful—you can predict where improvement is needed.

What advice would you give teachers considering making a change?

If you're so burnt out, broken, and disappointed from teaching, go somewhere you don't care for a bit and make money because leaving teaching can feel like you're always fighting the last war. *If you focus on passion, there is no income. If you focus on income, it's easy to have no passion. Get a job to sustain yourself, but keep working for the right role and culture/company fit for you, because teachers need passion.*

Meet my friend, Jennifer.

She's a former fifth and sixth grade teacher and administrator.
Today she's a business owner.

I met Jennifer through networking. Many years ago when I began this project, I knew I wanted to include other authentic experiences of those exiting the classroom. My cousin Carrie is a teacher so I asked if she knew of anyone who has successfully transitioned out and if they were open to sharing their experience. Enter Jennifer.

Turns out Jennifer's exit from public education wasn't from the classroom, but rather the pressures of being an administrator and the nearly impossible task of time commitments, stress, and supporting teachers who were reeling from their own traumas of teaching. Sadly this created a perfect storm of negativity.

When did you know you wanted a change?

I left the classroom because I felt a calling to serve in a new capacity—administration. In November my first year as a principal, I ended up in the ER with symptoms of a heart attack (tingling in my right arm, chest pains, severe headaches...). *After running all the tests, the doctors said, it's just stress.* It didn't get better. I continued to work 10–16-hour days, I pulled away from my husband and friends. In November the following year, I was contemplating suicide. At that same time I was told I would not have the unanimous vote from the school board for rehire. I chose to turn in my resignation. It was honestly a relief.

I took a new assistant principal position with the hope it would be different. Unfortunately, the teachers in the building had experienced collective trauma multiple times. This produced guarded personalities and deceptive behaviors by some of the teachers. It was another negative environment. The students, parents, and many of the faculty and staff were wonderful, but it was still the select few

notes

that made me dread coming to work. *I missed my family, I missed my friends, I missed my hobbies, I didn't know my husband anymore, and I missed me the most.* Instead of allowing their negativity to affect me as it had in my previous district, I decided to leave public education. So, I resigned in February of 2020 and began my own business.

What do you do now? Do you leverage any of your classroom skills?

I own my own franchise business. I had been saving my money and talking with my husband about leaving. It was what was best for me, my mental health, my marriage, and my children.

After researching franchise opportunities, I found a business model that was the perfect fit. We made our initial investment in the franchise early 2020. That was a scary decision as we were watching COVID-19 begin to cross our borders. My husband and I spent a lot of time in prayer, but decided it was the right decision to move forward.

With the franchise, I am able to use my strength in teaching, my administrative background, and one of my most loved hobbies. It was the best decision I could make. The growth of the business has been great considering we began a business during a pandemic. I have replaced my teacher pay, and I am working to grow the business to match, then exceed my administrator pay.

What advice would you give to someone also looking to make this change?

When you make the decision, *commit to it*. Do not allow the "what ifs" to take over. Just look forward and keep moving. You will hit roadblocks, stall out with growth occasionally, have hard weeks, and battle self-doubt. *While experiencing those things are tough, I also found freedom, financial opportunity, and better mental and physical health, and strengthened my marriage.*

Meet my friend, Shannon.

She's a former multi-grade international teacher (Thailand and South Korea). Today she's a sales enablement specialist and small business owner.

Another networking connection! Shannon is a ball of energy and I felt her presence at a conference we were both at. Again, not sure how it came up, but it usually does once you start talking about who you are and your background, and we found out we were both former teachers.

Shannon is resilient. Not unlike me, her transition out of the classroom has had ups and downs, and poor fit of roles and companies, but she not only sticks with it to get better fits for her, she is an entrepreneur.

Why did you change your career and leave teaching?

I really enjoyed working with middle-school students, and multiple school years in a row they would move me, after the start of the sessions, to kindergarten. That was just not for me, my personality type. *It made me realize that my joy wasn't in teaching.*

I had a side business—I did meal prep for expats. I really loved it and it started to take off. So I decided to invest there, and I went to the South Korean government to get a different visa. Instead of granting my request, they wanted to take my business from me and give it to someone who spoke more/better Korean. I said no.

I left teaching and the country and came back to the United States. And got into the hospitality industry.

What do you do now? What's been your career path since the classroom?

While in the hospitality industry, I became interested in sales and began pursuing an internal transfer. After many years of ups and downs, navigating company politics, and my manager passing from a heart attack, I left for an SDR/BDR role. Selling wasn't as engaging as I thought it would be.

However, I did find success in making sales training, playbooks, and refining processes for efficiency for my peers. This led to my realization that sales training and enablement is where I wanted to grow. I've invested my efforts here ever since.

What have been your most transferable skills from classroom to corporate?

Aside from our core teaching abilities, teachers are:

- Innovative problem solvers and creative. We can "figure it out" on the fly and present in a way that is quickly adaptable.
- Very organized. For example, I quickly created a library of gathered resources. This is something I did as a teacher and have done at each of my jobs since.
- Able to recognize the needs of people around us and efficiently address them.
- Hustlers. Teachers are natural hustlers in our work ethic. We get it done.

What advice would you give to someone also looking to make this change?

Network with everyone you can. Learn all the kinds of jobs out there and if you no longer want to be around people, pursue data entry or "back office" jobs. It's okay to give yourself grace if you want to disengage for a bit from teaching, from the

notes

stress. Have others be your cheerleader and remind you that you are okay and to take it easy on yourself.

Have someone on the outside to help you but have someone else write your bio. Teachers have a tendency to overthink and be very hard on themselves and sometimes the best description of us comes from those who care about us.

Learn to negotiate. You do it with parents (the list of school supplies to bring to class). Have the same type of list of what a job is going to bring to your career.

Always keep a side hustle, an entrepreneurial spirit. I do massage therapy and have various hobbies that I sell on the side. I don't know how not to have a side hustle!

Understand your values and strengths, know what brings you joy. Start here in your research. *Then, don't stop trying. It's not easy, but you taught kids, you can do this. You can do anything.*

Meet my friend, Elsie.

She's a former high school Spanish teacher.
Today she's a marketing project manager and events coordinator.

I met Elsie through a former co-worker. When I got the Teams chat at work one day asking to meet with her, I jumped at the opportunity. Elsie was already doing what was needed to make a change. Asking folks she knew—even from yoga class—if they knew anyone who could help or that was hiring. I didn't make the first move though, Elsie did. She sent me a DM on LinkedIn and we set up the call in early spring. In her interview, she spoke about the skill of using spreadsheets. I remember talking about them when we first met and having the discussion about how she could translate her teaching experience into business stories. Before the start of the next school year, she was in her first non-teacher role and on her way to building a successful career in marketing.

When did you know you wanted a change?

I began thinking about leaving teaching in year eight. It was COVID and I, *unlike most of my peers, loved working remote!* I had embraced technology (I had earned a supplemental degree) and could not get enough of the flexibility. At the same time, I was conflicted because my entire identity was teaching. I struggled with boundaries and saying no so much in the beginning. Early on I was told that because I was young and single that I should be working on campus at 8 pm every night. The administration told me *I could handle it*. I also had some scary moments early on and looking back, there were always signs. Overall, there were not that many, but a student threw a desk at me and it hit me. I wasn't severely injured but it certainly made me pause and wonder if this was right for me.

When did you actually leave teaching?

It wasn't until year 10 when we went back to campus that I realized this was not going to work. Student behavior was poor, socially the students were behind, and it was messy. Second, I was tired of the commute and sitting in traffic.

Not only that, I had wanted to change my personal life and invest more in my relationship. My boyfriend and I were buying a home and moving in together and due to the inflexibility of the school day, it made the final steps of the sale exceptionally difficult and we almost lost the house because I was not available during the workday. I got tired of not being able to live my life.

What do you do now? What's been your career path since the classroom?

I first got into marketing as a project manager at a very small company where I worked in an embedded role within clients' marketing departments. I had to learn a lot fast but I learned so much. It was because of this job that I got the job I have now that I enjoy much more. However, I could not have gotten this better-fit job for me without the great experience and the knowledge I learned from the first job. My first role was a very important stepping stone.

What have been your most transferable skills from classroom to corporate?

Number one is relationship building. My first manager told me she had never seen anyone build positive relationships with clients so fast. To me, this is what teachers do. We have to quickly build trust and a relationship with students.

Spreadsheets! Full transparency though, I did not do this enough as a teacher. I wish I would have pulled student data into a spreadsheet or Google Sheet and played around with it to get comfortable with them. I use them all the time in my marketing roles and they are no longer intimidating!

My additional degree in technology has helped a lot. I also worked at the state level. I spent planning, recruiting, and running Spanish immersion camps as well as writing curriculum and assessments (all for FREE. Looking back, I can't believe I gave all that time and energy for no pay!)

Others include:

- Agility and quickly learning new information.
- Organization and time management (this has been huge!).

notes

- Scaffolding and breaking down leadership strategy into a tactical plan for the client.
- Writing and content creation.

What advice would you give to someone also looking to make this change?

Don't be embarrassed or afraid to tell people you want a change. Talk to everyone about it; people are very willing to help and it's how I was able to make the right connections. I also went to career fairs and that is how I got my first job.

And don't make this big change alone. Lean on your support system to help you; a friend, loved one, or family member. It's a big deal and making the change alone would be really, really hard. Especially if you have children or are pregnant, it can be really hard, so have someone to support you and encourage you.

Last, don't shy away from a stepping stone job. It may not be the exact, best fit for you where you love everything. But if it gives most of what you are searching for (be it flexibility, remote work, PTO, benefits, etc.), then take it and learn as much as you can. It is that first job out that gets you the confidence and experience you need to move up!

Meet my friend, Tracey.

She's a former middle school language arts teacher.
Today she's a director of sales enablement.

I met Tracey when I was a solution consultant and my company wanted to sell our solution to Tracey and her company. Tracey was what you will learn should you pursue a sales rep path as a "champion." Champions are folks who mutually agree on the fit of the solution; they sell internally for you because they are the best at knowing their company needs (obviously). Because of my role, I was there to support her, get her questions answered, and ensure she had everything she needed for conversations with her leaders. I will say, the best part about sales is developing relationships with your customers. I was lucky enough to hit it off with Tracey and we stayed in contact.

It will come as no surprise when I gush about how talented Tracey is and how much I learned from her. I was not that far out of my teaching career when we met and it was neat to watch her navigate internal business. I wanted to be like her. She guided her company in buying a solution and liaised with us. I was impressed! When I learned she, too, was a former teacher, I was over the moon! I felt like I could be successful like her too.

Why did you decide to leave teaching?

I couldn't make ends meet. I had three kids and my partner wasn't working. My teacher salary could not support a family of five.

What steps did you take to leave teaching and find a new job?

I looked in the newspaper! I saw that Merryll Lynch was seeking teachers due to our skillset. In my interview, I was asked how I was going to balance my job and my children when they got sick. My retort: *would you ask a man that question?*

It wasn't easy. I had to work a lot harder than those around me. I was a woman, was older, and had kids. I had family and friends look over my resume and role play/practice with me, and I attended any company training sessions I could. I also read A LOT. I remember reading *You Are the Product*.

What have been your most transferable skills from classroom to corporate?

Pivoting to a new career was surprisingly easy for me because of my skills:

- Organize, track a budget, and run events.
- Communication and keeping attention of your audience.
- Read your audience; teachers can tell if they are "not getting it."
- Ability to multitask (this is huge).
- Creativity and problem solving.
- Quickly learn new content. Teachers are great at reinventing themselves.
- Make training engaging, fun, and measure the learning taking place.

What advice would you give to someone also looking to make this change?

I didn't do enough networking. You have to get to know people so you can get a new job and then advance once in the job. Find what you have in common with colleagues (knowing and playing golf has helped me immensely. It's not just a male hobby, ladies!)

Leaving can be scary, staying is even scarier. Don't apologize for taking a chance. If it doesn't work out, you can always go back to teaching; it can be a safety net.

notes

Summary of Themes

The value of networking cannot be underestimated. It is powerful. It is how you will get a conversation, an opportunity, an interview, or a job offer.

Is change scary? Yes! What's worse? Complacency. Staying in a job you hate. Staying where you are unsupported, unhappy, and exhausted cannot be your future.

Invest in yourself. Take time to assess your values and your strengths and even if you don't know exactly what you want to do, *be very clear on what you don't want.*

You have an incredible number of transferable skills for the corporate world. Simply take the time to learn how to explain them using corporate lingo and work on your business acumen.

Company culture is HUGE. You'll find yourself, maybe, in a company not fit for you. This does not mean you made a mistake exiting the classroom. Learn from the experience and find a better fit because you've already accomplished the hardest part—leaving the classroom.

Continue to network even after you get the new job. Promotions and opportunities will continue to come your way if you continue to find folks who believe in you and advocate for you (especially when you are not in the room).

> **Never forget: you are a professional and you belong here.**

LEARN THE LANGUAGE OF BUSINESS TO BUILD YOUR ACUMEN

Glossary

To begin a new career outside of teaching, it will be critical that you act as if you need to learn a new language. Business jargon can be buzzy, unfamiliar, and confusing, not unlike learning a new language! No one will expect you to be an expert, but like learning a new language, having the basics down will help you assimilate quicker into your new organization and working environment. As frustrating as learning this new skill may be, you have to. I find myself explaining rather often that businesses will not learn classroom and teacher jargon. Teachers must be the ones to learn to communicate their skills the way businesses can understand and receive the information.

Because I do still love the practice of teaching, I've put together a glossary of terms—pretty much what I used to make for my students or what we would make together for the entire class's benefit.

Keep in mind, jargon can be unique to each company. I'm sure you have been in one environment where they referred to something as one thing, and then went to another environment where the same item or process was called something else.

Others' definitions might differ, or some may think I left out some really important terms or parts of a definition. That's okay. These are the ones that have come up over the last several years of mentoring teachers, but certainly get other people's opinion on what terms are most important, what they mean, and why.

At the end of the glossary, you should add your own terms while you Google and spend time researching companies, industries, and careers. There are blank entries for you to use.

notes

Annual Operating Plan (AOP): An AOP combines the company strategy, roadmap, and objectives with managing the resources (investing vs. spending). Obvious and very important resources are cash (on hand), revenue (new cash), and expenses. The AOP can determine how much can, or should, be spent on what (including hiring).

Benefits Package: This is not just a health plan, vision, and dental. Benefit packages are so much more and almost all are negotiable when offered a job. Benefits are things like offering an FSA or HSA in addition to a medical plan. Benefits can be stock awards, RSUs, signing bonuses, 401(k) and contributions/match, car rental perks, vacation or paid time off (PTO), tolls/parking/public transit reimbursement, parental leave, food stipends/paid meals, performance prizes/SPIFs/incentives, etc. One overlooked benefit? Negotiating severance.

Board: Boards are formal groups of people that help steer a business in strategy and decision making. Some boards are made up of majority stockholders (both in privately held and publicly traded companies). A board in a business environment is not dissimilar to a school board. Both types have decision-making power or influence. Some boards are for advisory (advice giving) purposes only.

Business to Business (B2B): When a company sells products and/or services to other businesses. Ex: A car manufacturer selling pickup trucks to a construction company.

Business to Consumer (B2C): When a company sells products and/or services directly to consumers. Ex: You going to Target to buy paper clips or you purchasing Spotify.

Budget: You're probably familiar with this term. Why it matters in business is when a person, team, or department at a company wants to spend money, part of the process is determining if this new spend is in the budget. Asking if this spend fits refers back to the AOP. Hiring new folks to join the company makes a big impact on the AOP and these decisions, especially in down market years, are highly scrutinized.

Coder: Also referred to as a developer, these talented folks write code. Code can be in many languages and it's the basis of building software, web applications, and mobile apps.

Common Stock: Owning a share of common stock means you own a piece of the company, also called equity, in a publicly traded company. People who own stock are called shareholders which means you have voting rights when decisions are made.

Commission (also referred to as Incentive or Variable Compensation): Payments made to an employee for hitting a performance goal. Almost always used for revenue (think sales) roles. This is money earned above and beyond a base salary. Commission is paid based on how close you were to meeting a goal, meaning you don't have to hit 100% to get commission but the amount paid will be impacted by how close you are to meeting the set goal.

C-Suite: The leadership team with "chief" in their title. It means they lead the function and are the ultimate decision maker. Within the chiefs, there is a hierarchy with the CEO—Chief Executive Officer—being at the top. They are held accountable by the board members. Other common C-suite titles:

Chief Revenue Officer (CRO): leads all revenue, meaning sales, account management, and sales teams.

Chief Marketing Officer (CSO): leads all marketing efforts; sometimes this includes the BDR/SDR functions as well.

Chief Product Officer (CPO): leads product development and product marketing.

Chief Information Security Officer (CISO) or Chief Technology Officer (CTO): leads all IT, compliance, and security regulation functions internally and for customers if part of the solution or product offered by the company.

Chief Operations Officer (COO): runs the day-to-day operations of the company.

Chief Finance Officer (CFO): leads the accounting and finance organizations within the company.

Chief People Officer (CPO): leads the people productivity functions of a company. It is still common to refer to this department and efforts as Human Resources.

Earnings Report: Public companies must report to their shareholders how the company is performing. Their earnings are what gives the stock a monetary value per share. Private companies do not have to do this. Typically found in an investor section of the website, these reports can be long and a bit confusing to read but even the untrained eye can see if a company is in good health or not. There is also usually a summary that will tell you plenty without reading the entire document. This can be a helpful tool when researching companies to determine if joining would be positive due to success or more of a risk if the company is continuously underperforming.

notes

EBITDA: This is an acronym for Earnings Before Interest, Taxes, Depreciation, and Amortization. A lot to unpack here, but simply, this is also an indicator of a healthy, positive performing company and it's a way investors can measure if they should/not invest in a company. It's not always easy to know these details of a company's EBITDA as they do not need to be shared in a simple format; however, it can be calculated by reading earnings reports. I do not suggest spending that much time on it, but knowing what matters to a company when it comes to revenue and what is considered to determine profitability is very helpful when transitioning from the classroom to corporate.

> **Earnings Before:** Profits, revenue, and basically all the money coming into a company for sold products and services to consumers or buyers. The raw number before any deduction is made including obligations where a company owes money to another entity.
>
> **Interest:** Most businesses have loans that include interest, no different than us.
>
> **Taxes:** Again, just like us, companies pay taxes and at a higher rate than citizens.
>
> **Depreciation:** This is how a company spreads the cost of an item, a physical asset, over its lifetime. Companies do this for tax purposes, managed by the accounting team. Here's an example: A landscaping company buys 10 new work trucks and pays $500,000. The company doesn't let half a million in spend hit the books all in that one year. Rather they will spread out the cost of these 10 trucks over the lifetime of the truck and that half a million spend is spread out over the next 15 years.
>
> **Amortization:** Another accounting practice, similar to depreciation but rather than tangible items like work trucks, the value of a loan is spread out.

All this EBITDA talk is to simply get you familiar with knowing what matters to a company in regard to calculating profitability from generating revenue. It matters because *usually* healthy, profitable companies have a plan, strong leaders, and a great culture. These are the companies you want to work for, the companies that will be hiring, have better benefits/OTE, and can provide job security (less risk of a RIF).

Employee Stock Option Program (ESOP): Keeping in mind that benefits are beyond health insurance, businesses can award (give) stock to an employee in lieu of cash. Some companies give shares, others match what an employee buys.

Caution here is to know if the company is healthy (refer to those earning reports) and has a plan because companies will use stock value to replace cash performance bonuses, signing bonuses, 401(k) contributions, etc. It's a gamble, so mitigate your risk with research. Bets on stock have swung both ways for people—big gains, big losses.

Equity: When you are given a stake in the company's value. Depending on the company type, this would be RSUs or common stock (both are addressed in this glossary).

Fiscal Year: Companies don't always calculate profitability on a calendar year. For example, as citizens, our year begins on January 1. A company may not have a "start" to their year until April 1. This can help mitigate holidays overlapping with closing the financial books. Hiring cycles can follow this for companies because if a new hire can't be onboarded until the new budget starts, well, that may not mean January 1. Either way, the two most common fiscal years to start new budgets and start dates do not align with a school year.

Financial Planning and Analysis (FP&A): Planning here is the key word. This is the strategic function a company uses to determine if they can afford to hire people, give promotions, buy software, buy tools, buy vehicles—any expense. It is the day-to-day reference on spends, looking at what revenue is to come (forecast), and supports decision making, leading indicators. EBITDA and earnings reports are the look-back, lagging indicators.

Funding Round: Stages startup companies go through as they create value and get VCs to invest in their future. Angel investors are the first contributions a startup receives. As the company grows, they will receive or at least ask for rounds of funds that are in alpha order. Ex: A job posting may tell you this is a C-stage startup. This means they have had three rounds of investing, and they are early on. E and F rounds of funding are later. These companies should be on the brink of being self-sustainable with profits and would be ready for IPO and open for public investment.

Go-To-Market (GTM): This is part of a company's strategy to acquire new customers and keep current customers based on the product or service they have to offer. It is the plan of how they will message or speak about the product or service, why it matters for customers, who else might do what they do (address competition), and who is the ideal customer.

Headquarters (HQ): The main office location of a business.

notes

Hiring Manager: An employee of the company, most likely who will be your direct manager or the department leader your manager reports to.

Implementation: The process of setting up the client with the product or service they purchased. It may include training, technical setup, and ongoing support in the first days or months of using the new product or service.

Initial Public Offering (IPO): Becoming a public company, common stock is for purchase. When a company goes public, a value is given to RSUs and employee equity. Facebook went IPO at almost $40/share making thousands of early hires millionaires overnight. On the flip side, WeWork, who flubbed up their first IPO attempt, eventually went public with new investors at just over $10/share.

Leadership Team or Executive Leadership Team (ELT): The group of executive leaders just below the C-suite on the company hierarchy. Depending on the company and industry, the leadership team can be comprised of EVPs (executive vice presidents), SVPs (senior vice presidents), or any other high-ranking employee.

Learning Management System (LMS): An online application (web or mobile) to deliver training and content to employees. Some LMS companies have a business version of their software as well as an education version. A good example is the company Instructure. Canvas is sold to school districts; Bridge is sold to businesses.

Non-Disclosure Agreement (NDA): A binding agreement of terms agreed upon by both parties. If this is with a company and you are the employee, those make up both of the parties. This agreement can cover many topics, but the basis of the agreement is that you acknowledge that you will not discuss an event or matter outlined in the agreement. If you or the other party violate this term, there is usually a consequence or punishment (usually monetary) for violation.

Non-Compete Agreement: This clause is usually found in onboarding paperwork and is a way for a company to ensure an employee will not leave and go work for a competitor, will not convince clients to come to a new company, and will not support former clients at your new place of work. These clauses have term limits, usually one to three years.

Onboarding: The processes and procedures to bring on a new employee. From HR's perspective, this is standard paperwork (filling out a W2, sharing banking information for payroll, taking care of signing policies on behalf of the compliance/legal department). From IT's perspective, this will be getting you a laptop, email address, and your log-ins. From your department's perspective, this should include learning and coaching of the skills, processes, and company knowledge you'll need to be successful. Onboarding is very important. Before agreeing to join a company, you should ask about their onboarding process and program. If it sounds weak, it will be hard for you to get up and running. If it's robust and follows a clear path, you can be successful faster.

On Target Earnings (OTE), also referred to as Total Target Compensation (TTC): This is your entire benefits package. This is the amount of money you can expect to make in a year. Of course you will earn a salary, but OTE adds in expected income from performance or other bonuses, variable compensation awards, commissions and incentives, and any other financial contribution the company makes to you in a calendar year. If you are in sales, Winner's Circle or President's Club are common names for a company-paid vacation for performing the highest.

Private Equity (PE): A firm of people or companies that invest in companies. Value is held in stock but is not publicly traded. PE-backed companies do not have to publish earnings reports. It can be very hard to tell if a PE company is healthy or stable.

Product: What a company sells to generate revenue. Products can be a tangible item such as a car or roof shingles or intangible items like software, such as a mobile app (e.g., a music streaming service) or a web-based app (e.g., an online video game).

Publicly Traded Company: Shareholders own through stock corporate profits and assets.

Quality Assurance (QA): Testing that is done by the company, the client, and/or the end user to ensure all is working as expected before rolling out to a larger audience. If not working as expected, the project goes back into development to fix the issues, then QA testing will be repeated until acceptance is complete.

Quota: A numeric gauge of how many units, or dollars, an employee is asked to contribute to the company revenue target. These are usually only applied to revenue (think sales) generating roles.

Recruiter: A resource meant to find candidates for open roles. Most recruiters work for outside firms and are contracted by companies to find candidates and manage the screening process. If they are not directly employed by the company for which they are sourcing candidates, that will probably be evident in email address and LinkedIn profile.

notes

Reduction In Force (RIF): Layoffs. Most companies have had to RIF employees at some time or another. They are part of the corporate world. Companies with frequent RIFs are not healthy and you should avoid them.

Restricted Stock Unit (RSU): The restriction comes from the fact that until vested, the shares are not owned by the employee. It's a promise of future ownership if you stay with the company and in good standing. Companies can have their own policies and vesting requirements. Here has been my experience with earning RSUs and how they vest—it was the same at 3 different companies, so fairly standard. Say my compensation package included 1,000 RSUs. After one calendar year I would vest 25% (250). Then each month I would vest an equal amount of the remaining over a four-year period (~20 shares a month for the next 36 months). Once the RSUs are vested, they need to be purchased by the employee for a strike price. This is where people really make money in tech.

Return on Investment (ROI): This common phrase is used by companies to determine if they will get their money back plus additional revenue for spending money. It is a cost ratio of net income to the investment made.

Software-as-a-Service (SaaS): A software offering provided to another business or customer as a managed service. For example, web pages you visit to pay your HOA dues or lawn care. You use the site, but you don't have to maintain, update, or fix it if it breaks.

Service (act): What a company sells to make profit. Services can come directly from the company selling the product. Ex: GoDaddy sells domains and website hosting (the product) and also front-end web developers to make websites for those without the skillset or time necessary to build said website (a service). Services can also be acts such as consulting or landscaping.

Severance: Monetary compensation given to an employee who is laid off. These are negotiable for executive roles, but most people don't think to do so when going through the hiring process. Entry-level roles usually qualify for one week's pay for every calendar year worked. Again, don't shy away from severance questions and negotiating.

Single Sign On (SSO): A way to have one login ID and credential to get into multiple applications (web and mobile). An example is using your Google or Facebook information to log into your Spotify account.

Strike Price: The dollar amount an employee pays to buy their equity. Working in high tech, people expect to buy shares at less than a dollar to a few dollars as the company matures and grows pursuing IPO.

notes

Traditional IRA and Roth IRA: Supplemental retirement accounts. You add money after you've paid your taxes on those earnings. When you pull this money out at retirement age, you do not pay taxes on this money (pay taxes now, not later). There are annual contribution limitations and there is a salary cap to contribute to a Roth IRA before moving to an IRA. You can open these with any financial company. Ex: A lot of teachers contribute to a 403(b). A Roth IRA and IRA are similar.

Venture Capital (VC): A person, group of people, or collection of companies who pool their money or invest individually in companies. You've probably heard that startup companies are looking for funding. This is where the money comes from.

Waterfall: How your equity is distributed. This is a common method by which your RSUs or stock are awarded over time. This can be varied by company, but a common waterfall is earning 25% of your equity after working one calendar year from your start date. Then an equal percentage of the remainder every month for the subsequent years in the waterfall.

W9: Like a W2 but for 1099 Contractor (non-employee) work.

1099 (Contract Work): Not an employee of a company. Usually, short-term work with higher hourly or fixed fee for work. Flexible hours and as the hired expert you have discretion in how you solve the problem you were hired for. You do not qualify for employee perks or benefits.

401(k): How you contribute to a retirement account when not in the public sector. Companies with good benefits for employees will offer this (the company pays the fee for you to have one). Really good companies will offer a contribution or match a percentage of your employee contribution. *I highly recommend contributing at least enough to fully capitalize on the company's match rate. It's essentially free money and an easy way to boost your retirement savings.* Your contributions happen before you pay taxes on your paycheck. The perk is that you get to add money to retirement before taxes are taken out of your pay. However, you will pay taxes on this money when you retire. There are maximum annual contribution limitations, but you should always strive to max it out annually.

Acknowledgements

This book has been a long time coming for me. I took my first notes of what I was experiencing leaving teaching and building a new career in early 2016. From then on writing was in fits and starts: new jobs, moving, family needs taking priority. What never seemed to stop, though, was the steady outreach from strangers and intros from my network to talk to teachers who were unhappy and wanted a change or were at least considering a change. All the conversations had similar elements:

- Exhausted and burned out.
- Classroom challenges were too high, seemingly too great to overcome.
- Broke with no end in sight, retirement meant continued employment in some capacity.
- No support, and fear of retaliation from the school and other teachers.
- Where should they even start?
- An incredible amount of fear and self-doubt.

What a mess.

I'm grateful to have stumbled across Zach at Juxtabook in October 2023. By this time, I had been writing (I use the term loosely!) for six years. I knew the time was right because the flow of "help this teacher I know" requests were becoming more frequent. With Zach's help, I did in less than three months what I was unable to do on my own all those years.

Aside from being proud of myself for finishing a project that I care about, for fulfilling a personal goal and expectation of my very own, I'm excited for how this book might help change the lives of others who want a change but don't know how or where to start.

I'll be 40 soon and I've been asking myself, what is my legacy? I made it out of teaching and built a successful career in corporate America. I have started my own business since then too. But it nagged at me: what am I leaving for others? This book is that for me. I want to help, I want to make a difference, and I want to inspire teachers to invest in themselves and make a change. To go for it!

I do believe that teaching matters. I know it's an honorable profession, an exceptionally necessary one. I also feel that it is not an individual's job to sacrifice their life and livelihood if they are truly unhappy. I hope one day politicians can take a back seat to what students—and teachers—really need. Until then, I'll continue my efforts to help those that want to leave teaching make a career change.

I'll finish with a heartfelt thank you to my husband, James; my parents, David and Lisa; and my brother, Michael. I am so fortunate to have this group of loved ones around me, who encourage me, who love me. There isn't really anything I've achieved in my life that has not come to fruition without their love and support.

about the Font

I have always admired my grandmother's handwriting. Same for my Great Aunt Judy's. As I got older at family gatherings, they'd write me out a copy of their recipe for whatever yummy dessert or Jello salad they made. Every time, their handwriting would be immaculate. It would be this beautiful, yet legible, flowing script. It was classic teacher handwriting.

In this book I wanted to capture the connection I and my family have to teaching. I have several cousins and the spouses of cousins who are teachers. My dad's mother and several of my great aunts, all teachers. When I realized this project of mine, this guidebook was real and would be able to be published, I immediately wanted the title in my grandmother's classic script. But all I could think of was how sad it was that she passed and having her write for me was not possible.

My grandma, Mrs. Philipps, in the mid-1950s. This was taken around the time she would have just begun her teaching career.

My friend Justin was able to help make my dream a reality. He took old recipes and notes my dad had of hers and turned it into a font: *Mrs. Philipps*.

Her handwriting is used in the cover title and in several headings throughout the book. I love it. I love that a part of my family and our ties to teaching are captured in this guidebook. Teaching is an honorable profession. I'm glad there are teachers who stay if they really love the classroom.

My grandma's school photo from the early 1980s.

A class photo from early in her career, around 1955. Every student signed their name on the back of the photo.

My grandma's kindergarten class photo (1992-1993).

My grandma in her classroom with her students in the mid-1990s. This would have been one of her last years before retiring.

Personal Statement
(a note on the text)

I chose to be honest in the telling of my experiences as a teacher and in my several corporate roles. I did this so I could help others learn from my experiences. Like many others before me, I seem to have learned the most from my hardships, my disappointments, and even my mistakes. Not every experience in life, personally and professionally, is positive. That isn't unique to me, that's just life.

I wrote about my personal and professional experiences as I remember them: what it felt like in the moment, what it felt like immediately after, and even how I've processed them and the lasting impact each experience has had on my life and my career. Some of the names and identifying details in my stories have been changed to protect identities. Some events have been compressed, and some dialogue has been recreated to the best of my memory.

I realize some of the people in my story may wish events could have played out differently. They may recall the situations differently than I describe. Most events involve more than one person. How an event or series of events makes each of us feel is an authentic individual experience of emotions, reactions, and lasting impact. I can confidently say that I am sharing my experiences as truthfully and authentically as I recall them. The same goes for the teachers I interviewed. These stories are their authentic experiences and how they felt and how they remember them.

This work depicts actual events in the life of the author and interviewees as truthfully as recollection permits.

ashleyPhilipps
CAREER CHANGE CATALYST

Don't make the journey out of the classroom alone!

Join the community and get additional support.

"You are wonderful. I really can't thank you enough. So many aha moments and I feel confident in my plan moving forward."

–Katy, *current teacher seeking a career change*

Share a picture or video of the Now What? exercise that helped you the most and tag or @mention The Teacher's Guide to Changing Careers on LinkedIn or Instagram for **15% off your next purchase**.

DM @teachersguidetochangingcareers or email ashley@teachingcareerchange.com with the link to your post to receive your special discount.

Get social with us!